COPTIC ORTHODOX PATRIARCHATE

See of St. Mark

TEN CONCEPTS

BY

HIS HOLINESS POPE SHENOUDA III

Title   : Ten Concepts

Author   : H. H. Pope Shenouda III

Translated by : Dr. Wedad Abbas

Illustrated by : Sister Sawsan

Typesetting   : J.C.Center - Heliopolis

Press   : Dar El Tebaa El Kawmia, Cairo

Edition   : First - August 1994

Legal Deposit No : 8600/1994

Revised   : COEPA 1997

H.H. Pope Shenouda III
117th Pope and Patriarch of Alexandria and
the See of St Mark

CONTENTS

INTRODUCTION

Concepts often differ in our present time:

Everyone expresses his own views and there might be a contradiction among these different views, whether from writers, academics, philosophers or others... This may lead the young and the old to confusion and inquire - what is the truth?

So, this book is issued to be part of the curriculum taught in church education and Sunday School.

In this book, we speak to the youth about the concept of power, its sources, its characteristics: the power of the spirit, the power of the self, will-power, power of the nerves, power of the personality as a whole, power of prayers, power of faith ... for power is not confined to physical power! ...

We speak also about freedom; its concept and limits and how freedom is not absolute but should respect others' rights and observe law and public order as well as God's Commandments... It is such inner freedom released from faults and not harming itself.

In this book we explain also the concept of rest and fatigue, and how the body might suffer to make the spirit content and the conscience peaceful, and how a person might work hard to give others comfort. The concept of bodily rest and eternal rest is also explained.

The book explains the concept of ambition - whether it is wrong or right.

The concept of sin, its danger and impact on a person are explained here.

The book clarifies the concept of offense, what may be deemed offensive; whether offense is a cause for sin, and leads to and facilitates sin, even when a person might not be guilty of offending others; as well as what the sources and kinds of offense there are.

There is also an explanation of the concept of love and friendship, and the difference between love and lust, and the true friendship which does no harm.

The book tells also about the concept of meekness; its importance; the difference between meekness and tenderness; the relation between meekness and courage; and the cases in which one loses one's meekness.

The Concept of truth with all its meanings is also explained in this book; it speaks about the danger of half-facts, the relation between truth and justice, protecting others rights, the significance of defending truth and how this can be effected. It also states that truth is God, and whoever goes astray from truth, goes astray from God.

The book concludes with a chapter dealing with knowledge: whether useful or harmful knowledge.

Finally we pray to God that this book will be fruitful for the benefit of our people and children.

Pope Shenouda III

CHAPTER ONE

THE CONCEPT OF POWER

Power is of course a desirable attribute. Every one likes to be powerful and God's children are supposed to be powerful.

To speak about the concept of power, we shall deal with the following points:

Power is one of God's attributes:

- In the Trisagion we say, "Holy God, Holy Almighty..."

- In the Pascha Hymn we say, "Thine is the power and the glory... "

- We conclude the Lord's Prayer with the words: *"For Yours is the kingdom and the power and the glory"* (Matt. 6:12)

- The divine inspiration, speaking about the Spirit of God, said, *"the Spirit of counsel and might"* (Is. 11:2). The creation process, the raising of the dead, and miracles are proofs of God's power.

Since God is mighty and we are created in His image and likeness (Gen.:27), then we are supposed to be mighty and powerful.

God is Almighty and He is also the source of true power:

That is why we sing in the Pascha Hymn the words of the psalmist, *"The Lord is my strength and song"* (Ps.118:14). So the divine inspiration says, in the Book of Zechariah the Prophet, *" 'Not by might nor by power, but by My Spirit', says the Lord"* (Zech. 4:6).

It is also stated in the Holy Bible, *"and God has chosen the weak things of the world to put to shame the things which are mighty"* (1 Cor. 1:27). But why?

St. Paul the Apostle says, *"that the excellence of the power may be of God and not of us"* (2 Cor. 4:7).

In order for God to be the source of our power, St. Paul the Apostle says, *"I can do all things through Christ who strengthens me"* (Phil. 4:13).

It is true that we wish to be powerful, but let God be the source of our power. He gives us power. Let us not depend on our own power but on His power. Let us stand before Him weak and take power from Him.

I remember once I wrote in my notes : Satan said to God, 'Leave the powerful to me, I am capable of dealing with them. As for those who feel their weakness, they resort to You God, and fight me with the power they take from You, so I can't overcome them'.

Sources of power:

Of course the main source of power is God alone, as the Lord said to His disciples, *"But you shall receive power when the Holy Spirit has come upon you"* (Acts 1:8), and St. Paul the Apostle said, ***"I can do all things through Christ who strengthens me"*** (Phil. 4:13).

Sources which people might mention with respect to a strong personality are : mind, soul, will and spirit - all these without God will be of no avail; for the Lord said, ***"Without Me you can do nothing"*** (John 15:5). But if God's power enters your life, it will appear in all such matters. So, ask God to give you the power that you may sing this beautiful hymn: *"The Lord is my strength and song, and He has become my salvation"* (Ps. 118:14).

Some people may wonder about the words of the Lord Jesus Christ to His disciples, *"he who believes in Me, the works that I do he will do also; and greater works than these he will do"* (John 14:12)! But there is an important essential difference :

The Lord Christ works miracles by His own power, but the believers work miracles by His power. The miracle worked by them might be very great, but it is not by their own power.

It is by the power of the Lord who works within them, who said, *"Without Me you can do nothing"* (John 15:5).

God's Children are supposed to be powerful, provided that God be the source of their power. They should not depend on, or take pride in, their own power.

This is an essential requirement for the power of God's Children.

Take for example David: undoubtedly he was weak if compared to Goliath the valiant who was boastful of his power, but David ascribed all his power to God. He said to that valiant, *"You come to me with a sword, with a spear, and with a javelin. But I come to you in the name of the Lord of hosts... This day the Lord will deliver you into my hand; for the battle is the Lord's, and He will give you into our hands."* (1 Sam. 17:45-47). Thus David won over Goliath, because Goliath fought with his human power, while David fought with God's power.

The spiritual persons, in all their works, ascribe power to God.

When St. Peter and St. John healed the lame man at the gate of the temple which is called Beautiful, people were filled with wonder and amazement at the miracle. So, the two saints said to them, *"why do you marvel at this? Or why look so intently at us, as though by our own power or godliness we had made this man walk?"* (Acts 3:12).

Then the two apostles drew people's attention to the Lord Christ whom they crucified, saying, *"through faith in His name, has made this man strong, whom you see and know... has given him this perfect soundness in the presence of you all"* (Acts 3:16).

God's power is unlimited and human beings are powerful through God.

When consecrating monks we read a chapter from the epistle of St. Paul the Apostle which says, *"Finally, my brethren, be strong in the Lord and in the power of His might. Put on the whole armor of God, that you may be able to stand against the wiles of the devil"* (Eph. 6:10,11), as if we say to them: You are about to enter into battle with Satan and his forces and you need power. The power which you need should be the divine power.

What then are the characteristics of this power which they should acquire ?

The power of the spirit:

Some young people think that power means bodily strength which wrestlers and other sports people have, or the kind of strength which Samson the Valiant had (Judg. 13-16).

However, bodily strength is not everything. Many of those who have bodily strength are weak spiritually.

Samson the Valiant who overcame many people through his bodily strength, was weak before the temptation of Delilah. He weakened before her and disclosed his secret to her, so she cut off his hair and delivered him to his enemies who plucked out his eyes, bound him with fetters and made him grind in the prison (Judg. 16:19-21).

And David who defeated Goliath the Valiant (1 Sam. 17) was from his boyhood, *"a mighty man of valor, a man of war"* (1 Sam. 16:18). This mighty man was weak before the beauty of Bathsheba, so he fell and sinned and deserved to be punished by God because he gave great occasion to the enemies of the Lord to blaspheme (2 Sam. 12:7-14).

Here we quote the words of St. John the Beloved to the youth in his first epistle: *"I have written to you, young men, because you are strong, and the word of God abides in you, and you have overcome the wicked one"* (1 John 2:14).

There is another kind of power, which is to overcome the wicked one (Satan)

The powerful person then, is the person who overcomes sin.

He who overcomes sin overcomes because God's word abides in him, and God's commandment abides in his heart. On the other hand a person who is overcome by sin cannot be powerful. He has a weak point through which the devil can enter and defeat him.

A powerful spirit overcomes the body, the material and the devil.

Whatever spiritual wars you face, you should resist even to bloodshed (Heb. 12:4), and seek God's assistance until you overcome, just as Joseph the righteous man overcame (Gen. 39).

A powerful spirit does not let itself be mastered to any habit, nor does it accept to be defeated, no matter how difficult the struggle may be, or how deceitful the devil may be. The spirit is more powerful than Satan's temptation, his deceit and his wiles.

A person who is overcomed by any habit is a weak person.

For example, a person who is overcome by the habit of smoking or drinking, or subjugated to addiction, is not a powerful person because he is weak before all such habits. He has no will power before these habits, but the habit or addiction has dominion over his will and his behaviour and may lead him to crime.

Self power:

A powerful person does not feel anxious or disturbed, nor does he experience fear, failure or hesitation.

His spirit is like the cataracts in the river, struck by waters and waves for years and centuries and remain fixed in their place, or like the mountains hit by winds, rains and floods without being affected.

Thus a person who is powerful in spirit says with David the Prophet : *"Though an army should encamp against me, my heart shall not fear; Though war should rise against me, in this I will be confident"* (Ps. 27:3).

A powerful person is steady and holds out against hardships and threats. He is powerful despite the external pressures.

On the other hand, the weak imagines fears and is disturbed because of this.

Such fears may probably have no existence! But due to inner fear, he expects troubles and becomes worried without reason !!

A powerful person does not set the possibility of failure or defeat in front of him; for St. Paul the Apostle said, *"For God has not given us a spirit of fear, but of power"* (2 Tim. 1:7), *"Therefore we do not lose heart"* (2 Cor.

4:16). Any fighting, troubles or hardships will not enter the heart and disturb it.

A powerful person deals with the troubles outside him, while a weak person allows them into his heart and nerves and is troubled by them.

This is the power of the spirit which the distinguished are characterized.

In an examination, the weak feel perplexed, sweats and faints when he finds a difficult question and forgets whatever he has learned !! But a powerful student thinks of the solution, by analyzing the question, and gains confidence to solve the problem.

In fact, the real concept of power ought to concentrate on internal power.

Some people may seem powerful from the outside while they are completely lost inside. Such a person may say, if insulted, "God forgive you", but within he is full of rage and hatred. The commandment of turning the other cheek (Matt. 5:39) is said by one of the saints to be the inner feelings, that is interior forbearance, forgiveness and blaming of oneself.

Interior power is also overcoming one's own self. The powerful is not he who overcomes others, but rather who he overcomes himself.

One of the saints said: Man is given the power of anger, not to use it against others and be angry with them but to use it against himself if he does wrong. It is well said in the Psalm, *"The royal daughter is all glorious within"* (Ps. 45:13). So, if you overcome your inner self, you can overcome any external matters, and you will be able to overcome all enemies. St. John Chrysostom says, 'No one can do harm to a person unless such a person does harm to himself.'

Among the Characteristics of power is self-control.

He who controls his tongue is a powerful person as said by St. James the Apostle (James 3:2). A great point of weakness, which we pay highly for, is the tongue which accuses.

A powerful person can control his thoughts so that they may not overcome him or cause him to stray and thus sin.

A powerful person controls himself at the time of anger and at the time of fasting with respect to food and drink, and controls himself with regard to time; he does not waste his time in enjoyment and entertainment and hence fails to carry out his spiritual responsibilities.

The power of the nerves:

Another kind of power is the power of the nerves.

A person with weak nerves becomes enraged and agitated over any small word. He loses his temper and self-control, his behaviour and words are offensive and he is an object of criticism by others because his nerves cannot bear the situation, though he may be powerful in other aspects.

Nerves in fact pertain to the body, but psychological factors have an influence, because a person who is subject to the sin of anger has his nerves quickly inflamed.

A person who is subject to self-love and dignity is sensitive to any word and thinks it has hurt his dignity and troubled his nerves because his nerves cannot endure.

Nerves are his point of weakness.

Therefore the apostle says, *"We then who are strong ought to bear with the scruples of the weak"* (Rom. 15:1). A person who attacks others is a weak person, while he who endures is strong, like a steady mountain that is not aroused by the offenses of others. Such a mountain remains fixed, not shaken regardless of the situation.

But a person who rages and tries to offend others is vanquished by himself not by others. A simple word might trouble him, make him lose his temper and destroy his nerves.

While the powerful has strong nerves and strong forbearance.

So, he who endures is powerful, and he who hurts others is weak.

Examine yourself to find out your weaknesses and do your best to overcome them.

The powerful is not the person who overcomes others, but he who can overcome himself. Many think themselves triumphant and powerful while they are weak and defeated within.

The powerful does not only bear the offenses but also bears occurrences and problems.

He bears the hardships which may worry others, and endures illnesses, afflictions and other hardships.

The Lord Christ was powerful in His forbearance, in bearing defiance while on the cross when they said to Him, *"If you are the Son of God, come down from the cross"* (Matt. 27:40). So we say to Him in the Divine Mass, "You have borne the oppression of the wicked".

Aggression is easy. Any person with a weak personality or weak character can attack others, but the powerful endures.

In marital life, if the couple are weak and cannot bear each other, they may destroy their home! But if one of them at least is powerful, he can bear with the other and so peace prevails between them.

A weak person may break down when hearing certain news. His nerves, his mind and his life are affected. His health cannot endure, his blood pressure rises, his heart fails and he may even collapse. He has no power to bear the news !! Another point is :

The power of love :

It is written in the Holy Bible, *"love is as strong as death ... Many waters cannot quench love, nor can the floods drown it"* (Song 8:6,7). Love is strong and positive, in that it gives and sacrifices, even sacrificing oneself for whom one loves...

Love is also strong with respect to the passive aspect, in that it endures the faults of others, regardless of what they may be. So the Apostle says, *"Love never fails"* (1 Cor. 13:8).

But a person who turns his love away from a friend because of a word or action, may be because his love initially was weak.

Love is capable of ascending to the cross in order to save and redeem.

Such strong love tolerated the denial of Peter, the doubt of Thomas, and the fleeing of the disciples at the time of arresting the good Master. Strong love extends to the enemies and offenders and blesses those who curse (Matt. 5:44).

The power of the personality:

A powerful personality is distinguished by strong mentality and thought.

When an person who has intelligence, understanding, discernment, eloquence, persuasiveness and good memory, deals with a particular matter, he supports his point of view clearly and in a way which is capable of attracting and convincing others.

He does not follow any rumor or belief, but thinks and examines the matter and holds fast to what is best. With his intelligence and understanding, he succeeds in any responsibility entrusted to him. Such a person stands strong in the face of any problem. He does not allow a problem to defeat him, but he solves it or bears with it until it is solved. A person who breaks down before any problem is not powerful.

A powerful personality does not obey any wrong counsel. A person with a powerful personality influences others and is not influenced by them except by the counsel of the spiritual. A powerful personality does not mean that a person be stubborn and opinionated. But rather, he is powerful in good deeds and simple in dealing with others.

Some people have strong influence over others. Those who are fit for ministry and leadership are unlike those who have poor minds, even though they may be physically strong or holding great positions, they cannot lead others who might be more intelligent and more opinionated. It may happen that someone faces a problem and refuses any advice and is not convinced by any words until a certain person speaks to him and influences him, so he accepts his advice. The words of such a person are powerful, effective and influential. They do not return void.

Such influential power is useful for spiritual guidance, for the ministry of preaching and for attracting others.

Such power is useful also with respect to friendship and social work. It is useful for those who hold management and leadership positions. It is good for a writer or journalist as such power would have its attractiveness and effectiveness.

Some persons are powerful in ministry and preaching.

They have the power of speech, influencing others and the ability to attract people to God. Their word does not return empty (Is. 55:11), but is fruitful. Such as St. Paul the Apostle, St. Mark, and St. Athanasius the Apostolic who confronted the Arians and spread the orthodox faith. Every spiritual priest has spiritual influence which is deep, like every preacher or successful minister.

Meekness does not contradict power. The Lord Christ was powerful and meek at the same time. He never quarreled or cried out (Matt. 12:19), but at the same time He was persuasive and had a strong personality that convinced His adversaries in every discourse.

The Will power:

One of the aspects of power in a person is their will power or resolution. When such a person wills anything, he can carry it out. When he takes an exercise for example, he begins and is capable of going on and completing it. On the other hand a weak person may have the will but not the capability. He may begin but does not continue.

Among the aspects of will power is self-control.

A powerful person can control himself whether at the time of anger or against the wish to revenge. He can also control himself against any lust or any sin fighting him. A powerful person can restrain his tongue, his senses and his thoughts. Suppose such a powerful person has diabetes, he will be able to restrain himself from forbidden foods.

Here I want to say: If a person cannot restrain himself from food in cases of disease or fasting, how would he be able to control himself against any lust or any sin ?

Some persons are weak before certain allurements.

These allurements might be position, money or lust. Before such things he cannot endure, he is overcome by his weakness or his lust and falls or deserts his faith!

Others might become weak before vain glory, or before words of praise and extolling. Martyrs and confessors, on the other hand, were very powerful before all allurements.

The power of prayers and faith:

Another kind of power is the power of prayers.

A prayer supported by the power of faith, zeal, humility and spirituality can ascend to heaven and find response.

People feel the power of a person who have such a way with prayer and resort to him to find solutions to their problems from God through him.

The prayer of the Apostles was so powerful that it was said, *"And when they had prayed, the place where they were assembled together was shaken; and they were allied with the Holy Spirit"* (Acts 4:31). This is the powerful prayer that ascends to heaven and is presented before God's throne and receives what it asks for.

Do you have such prayer which others may seek? You can read about it in the lives of saints.

A powerful prayer is spirited and full of faith.

Faith gives power to prayers, and the power of prayer with the power of faith work together.

With the power of faith St. Peter walked on the water, but when his faith was shaken he began to sink. The Lord saved him and said, *"O you of little faith, why did you doubt?"* (Matt. 14:31).

Powerful faith can work miracles. Suffice what the Holy Bible says, *"All things are possible to him who believes"* (Mark 9:2,3).

Elisha the prophet went with the Shunammite woman confident that he would be able to raise her son (2 Kin. 4:35).

Elijah the Prophet also did the same with the widow of Zarepath of Sidon and he raised her son (1 Kin. 17:22).

Powerful faith believes that the Lord will come even at the last watch of the night. Lazarus will rise even after four days of his being buried.

Your faith is unshaken even though God delays in responding, or the prayers seem not to be heard.

It is faith that doubts not God's love, though tribulations encompass or continue, and though plowers plow on his back and make their furrows deep (Ps. 129:3).

The power of faith does not only appear in trusting God's work, **but the power of faith appears also when confronting heretics**.

An example of this is the powerful faith of St. Athanasius who rejected the Arian thoughts and suspicions. The faith within his heart was stronger than their suspicions.

On the other hand, weak faith cannot withstand doubts or heresies and heterodoxies.

CHAPTER TWO
THE CONCEPT OF FREEDOM

In this chapter we shall present some concepts pertaining to certain matters relating to both spiritual and social life. Beginning with the Concept of Freedom, let us discuss it with our young people:

God likes everyone to be free:

God created man with a free will and said to him in the Book of Deuteronomy, *"See, I have set before you today life and good, death and evil ... I call heaven and earth as witnesses today against you, that I have set before you life and death, blessing and cursing; therefore choose life, that both you and your descendants may live, that you may love the Lord your God, that you may obey His voice, and that you may cling to Him, for He is your life"* (Deut. 30:15-20).

Freedom necessitates accountability and responsibility:

A person or any being who has no freedom is not accountable for his doings.

On the other hand, freedom necessitates the accountability of man for whatever he does whether good or evil so that he might be rewarded for his good works and punished for his wrong or evil works. Adam and Eve were free and when they had had God's Commandment they could have obeyed or broken it. But they broke the Commandment and God inflicted punishment on them (Gen. 3:9-19).

Punishment for a wrong doing of a person who has discretion is double: on earth and in heaven. He may escape punishment on earth but punishment remains in the other world not abolished except by repentance (Luke 13:3-5).

Likewise the reward for a good deed of a person done by his free will is a double reward. Even though a person does not obtain the reward on earth, it is kept for him in heaven, *"your Father who sees in secret will reward you openly"* (Matt. 6 :4,6).

You are not entitled to absolute freedom:

You are free to do whatever you want provided that you do not impose upon the rights or freedoms of others, nor break God's commandments or public order laid down for the safety and peace of others.

For example, you have no right to violate traffic rules while driving your car and say: I am free to go wherever I want !! Nor have you any right to raise your voice and make noise that is disturbing to others and say: I am free to raise my voice as much as I like !!

You have no right to cheat in exams from other papers and say : I am free to use whatever papers I like!!

As you ought to use your freedom in a way that does not harm others or violate the public order, you should also use your freedom in such a way as not to cause harm to yourself.

Your own self does not belong to us. It belongs to God who created it and redeemed it. It belongs also to the community that cared for you and brought you up and thus you have obligations towards it.

Therefore killing oneself in suicide is a crime which is punished by God and rejected by law. The same applies to whoever causes himself harm through smoking or drugs. Such a person cannot say: I am free to smoke whenever I like!! He has no right to destroy himself or deprive the community of his existence and from performing his duty towards it.

Restrictions against freedom are for your benefit :

Restrictions are useful in that they hold you back from doing harm to yourself, to others, or to the community and from breaking God's commandments.

A river has two banks, they do not restrain its watercourse but preserve it.

If a river has no banks it will flow on both sides and inundate the land turning it into swamps. I wonder if rivers object to having two banks and say : Banks restrain our freedom!!

It is the same for you; the banks to you are God's commandments, the laws and the traditions or perhaps religion and education. Both are for your benefit; for a child who refuses education and considers it restricting his freedom, or the youth who refuses the advice of his parents, his teachers or his guides, seeing in them a restraint to his freedom, such a person will be corrupt and will be led astray from the right path. Can straying be another name for freedom or a consequence thereof ?

Real freedom is to free yourself of your faults:

One should free oneself of faults, bad habits and bad feelings of the heart, and free one's mind of deviating thoughts. One should turn away from being subject to the devil and his supporters, from the influence of bad company and corrupt association and from every control over one's will intended to lead one astray.

Such is the freedom meant by the Holy Bible, *"If the Son makes you free, you shall be free indeed"* (John 8:36).

He who is freed from sin internally, can use external freedom in the right way:

For example he who is free from hatred, cruelty, violence and oppression, can use his freedom properly when dealing with people. But if a person is offensive or cold-hearted and wishes to use his freedom in whatever way he likes, he will hurt others with his cruelty and offensiveness.

Likewise, a person who is not freed from bodily lusts can abuse his freedom in harming others instead of using his freedom to preserve his purity and holiness.

A girl, for example, who says: I shall put on whatever dress I like, and laugh or enjoy myself as I want, is in this way offending others and may cause others to fall besides herself. Such a girl is not yet free internally, so she uses her external freedom in a way that causes harm to herself and to others.

A student who is not serious in his study all year and says: I am free to do whatever I want, is in fact doing harm to himself and is misusing his freedom, and thus cannot succeed in his life because he is not freed within from the domination of diversion.

My advice to you is, use your freedom for your own benefit and for the benefit of others. Free yourself within first before you practice your external freedom.

Some may restrain themselves to attain real freedom:

Such a person does not give himself whatever he wants lest he should spoil himself or lose control over himself and lose the real freedom.

So, such a person proceeds into spiritual training to control himself, restrain his tongue so that it might not err, control his nerves so that he may not rage and lose his friends. He proceeds also with spiritual exercises to control his thoughts so that they may not wander in harmful matters, as well as spiritual exercises to control his body through fasting and vigil and to control it regarding lusts so that he may not plunge into diversion and sensual delight and lose his spirituality.

Is it right for anyone to say: I shall behave as I wish, freely, and not restrain myself and force myself to do good? And if so, is such a person really free or dominated by his lusts?

CHAPTER THREE

THE CONCEPT OF REST & FATIGUE

Types of rest:

Rest is mentioned in the story of creation, in the beginning of the Holy Scriptures. It is said, *"Then God blessed the seventh day and sanctified it, because in it He rested from all His work which God had created and made"* (Gen. 2:3).

The rest meant here is the rest after finishing or completing work. When a person completes what he is doing he feels comfort and rest.

The Lord God rested on the seventh day from His work as the Creator.

He rested on the Sunday of the Resurrection after He had completed His work of salvation and redeemed people from sin and death.

Another type of rest is that expected by the world, that is, the eternal rest.

No fatigue, illness or suffering shall be there during this rest which lasts forever. All causes of worry shall cease to exist.

Some other rest that precedes the eternal rest is that experienced by people after death. A person after death rests from the troubles of this world, from the disturbance and the burden of the body, and from the evil existing around him, as the Holy Bible says, *"that they may rest from their labors, and their works follow them"* (Rev. 14:13).

That is why we say a departed person is in repose which means rest.

There are other kinds of rest while we are on earth. There is the physical rest, the rest of the mind, soul, heart and feelings as well as the rest of one's conscience. There is also psychological rest as well as spiritual rest. We shall deal with all this in detail, but let us begin with bodily rest.

The bodily rest:

God Himself willed that the body takes rest. He created the body and He knows its nature that it needs rest. So He gave it the seventh day of the week as the day of rest. He said about the Sabbath, *"The Sabbath was made for man, and not man for the Sabbath"* (Mark 2:27).

And concerning the holy days and feasts of the Lord, He said, *"You shall do no work on it"* (Lev. 23:3,7).

So, we should give the body physical rest, for it is not a sin but rather a divine commandment.

A person should be wise so as not to exhaust his body beyond its power nor give it more rest than it needs which leads to laziness or sluggishness.

I remember a professor of medicine in London who said to me: 'I cannot prevent you from hard work; for your responsibility requires that, but I prevent you from over work.' By 'over work' he meant work that is done after a person becomes exhausted and ought to have stopped. He said to me also: 'The work you do happily and joyfully will not injure your heart, whereas the work you do when feeling annoyed and troubled will exhaust you physically.' Feeling delighted in work makes one not feel tired.

There is a relation then between psychological or mental rest and physical rest.

An untroubled spirit can bear the burden of the body, but if the spirit is troubled, the body will feel tired. To make the body comfortable, as some scientists say, do not let it work for a long time without rest. Give your body some rest, even for a few minutes, amidst long hours of work. This is the purpose of the break given during work, to help your body recover and give you rest.

The body suffers also from illness and becomes unable to endure.

A sick person often needs complete rest. He gets tired if he talks or listens too much. He gets tired because of any sound, movement or thinking. For this reason, hospitals limit visiting hours. Do not think that you give comfort to the sick by your lengthy visits or endless talk!

Bodily rest is different from laziness.

Laziness means that a person has the ability to work but does not want to work. Laziness, therefore, has many consequences such as, the failure to carry out responsibilities. There is also the physical aspect which laziness may lead to, such as heaviness or sluggishness and hence the body loses its natural vitality. It may also lead to weight gain and apathy.

It is well known that humid weather leads to laziness, whereas cold weather helps one to be active and move. Movement also generates heat within a person. Therefore the retired who spend the rest of their lives at home or at the club become sluggish, while the retired who go on working remain physically powerful.

Likewise active, working women differ from those who sit at home doing nothing but become overweight and lazy.

By bodily rest we do not mean absolute rest.

The body might be fast asleep but the heart works regularly. So too the other systems of the body : the respiratory system, the brain and the other systems, all of them work during one's sleep and rest. What causes trouble to the heart or the brain is exhaustion not work.

Thus rest does not mean refraining from work completely, it may sometimes mean changing the kind of work. That is why rest in French is called "recreation", which means "to create again" as when the mind creates one thought after another.

Concentrating on one thought exhausts the mind.

So, when one gets tired of concentration, one ought to move to another thought. The mind is always thinking, but it gets tired of deep thinking on a certain subject for a long time and needs to leave it for sometime to return to it afterwards after having restored its activity.

Sometimes rest is connected with fatigue.

A person may need, for example, some exercises to keep his body healthy by activating it. Some people may achieve this by walking or running. Fatigue may be endured for physical benefit. However, what we mean is fatigue caused by physical therapy, not exhaustion.

Fatigue between the self and the spirit:

Some sick persons may feel bad when they know their case is dangerous, but they prepare themselves for their eternity and thus feel the comfort of the spirit.

Therefore people ought not to deceive a sick person making him think he is all right and entertain him with worldly means so that he may feel comfort, because he would neglect his spiritual life and eternity and may perish.

Another example is to flatter a sinner by saying he is right to give him peace of mind but in fact you cause him to perish, because he will not rebuke himself nor repent. The same goes with respect to flattering those in higher positions or spoiling children. Here we give an important spiritual rule:

If you cannot rebuke a sin, do not justify it.

By justifying the behaviour of sinners, you participate in their responsibility.

Jezebel encouraged Ahab to oppress Naboth the Jezreelite and take his vineyard, thus making him pleased, but she damaged him spiritually and deserved the same punishment.

Likewise a person who lies to get out of a critical situation, feels peace of mind but causes harm to his spirit. Also a person who swindles to attain some purpose gains the same result.

He who does not examine his conscience and rebukes himself for his sins feels comfort of mind but leads himself to perdition. Worse still is the person who tries to justify himself to feel comfort, for such comfort is false and sinful.

Among the cases of harmful rest is the case of a person who gains his own rest at the expense of the fatigue of others.

Such rest is a kind of selfishness and self-affection and lack of love for others. A person in this case gives comfort to himself while his spirit is burdened with faults.

Internal fatigue:

Some persons have no external reason for fatigue but fatigue comes from within them, from the concerns of the heart, anxiety, suspicions, fear and pessimism. Everything that happens to them causes them trouble; they are the cause of their own fatigue not others.

Clear conscience:

A person may endure physical fatigue to clear his conscience or spirit.

Martyrs and confessors, for example, endured many torments to the body in order to have clear conscience for being steadfast in faith.

Another example is the torturing endured by St. John the Baptist when he was put in prison and finally his head was cut off, because he testified to the truth and confronted the King saying, *"It is not lawful for you to have your brother's wife"* (Mark 6:18).

A similar example is the exile of St. Athanasius the Apostolic for defending the creed against the Arians.

Likewise, Joseph the righteous man endured prison to keep his conscience clear and pure. He said, *"How then can I do this great wickedness, and sin against God?"* (Gen.39:9).

Pastors also endure such fatigue of the body.

They endure so that people might be in comfort and also to clear their conscience that they are performing their pastoral work.

This applies to whoever takes the way of sacrifice, giving and being honest in their work. Such a person may feel tired physically but feels peace of mind, and comfort in spirit for performing his duties. He does not seek his own comfort but that of others.

Also the student who works hard, has a clear conscience with regard to his career and this makes him happy in spite of fatigue because he achieved peace of mind.

Likewise all those who struggle in fatigue and hard work for the purpose of achieving a goal, just as a poet once said, 'To achieve what great souls want, bodies must work hard.'

Even in spiritual struggling, a person should labour and fight a good fight to clear his spiritual conscience and to make his spirit rest in God. Therefore the Apostle said rebuking, *"You have not yet resisted to bloodshed, striving against sin"* (Heb. 12:4).

However, there are some people who tire their bodies and their spirits at the same time.

So, a spiritual person labours for the sake of righteousness, while a sinner labors in vain. Such vain labour resembles that of devils in their temptation of human beings.

Fatigue in the field of ministry:

A minister labours to clear his conscience and give comfort to others.

And as the Apostle says, *"each one will receive his own reward according to his labour"* (1 Cor. 3:8). Thus St.

Paul laboured in ministry for edifying the kingdom and for the salvation of the people.

A minister who does not labour physically for the sake of his ministry, will not feel comfort spiritually nor cause comfort to those whom he serves.

CHAPTER FOUR

THE CONCEPT OF AMBITION

Ambition:

Ambition is the desire for elevation and continuous aspiration.

Ambition is the case of a person who never feels satisfied and never stops at a certain level.

Now, is this wrong or right? Is it spiritual or not spiritual? Normal or abnormal? Should a person go that way or resist it? These are important questions to which we shall give answers here with regard to the kind of ambition and its direction.

Ambition is a natural thing, part of man's nature.

Man is created after God's image and likeness. But God is unlimited, how then can man be made in God's image with regard to this attribute in particular while God alone is the Unlimited? The answer is that:

God created in man the inclination to the unlimited.

Since man cannot be unlimited by himself; for being unlimited is the attribute of God alone, his desires and ambitions became inclined to an unlimited level . Whenever a person attains a certain position, he longs for a higher and better one. St Paul says to us, *"not to think [of himself] more highly than [he] ought to think, but to think soberly"* (Rom. 12:3). So, as long as man is created in God's image, ambition will be a natural thing in him.

However, ambition differs from one person to another.

According to the kind of ambition, it is deemed to be good or evil. Good ambition is a long way one must walk. There is a sentence before which, believe me my friends, I stand astounded and amazed: *"till we all come... to the measure of the stature of the fullness of Christ"* (Eph. 4:13).

The path towards perfection is long and its concept is so deep, we ought not to walk in it slowly or sluggishly but to follow the words of the experienced saint, *"Run in such a way that you may obtain it"* (1 Cor 9:24). He even applies this to himself saying, *"Therefore I run thus"* (1 Cor. 9:26).

I wonder whether this saint continued to run thus even after he had ascended to the third heaven.

Holy ambition then is spiritual ambition, aiming at a spiritual objective, and taking a spiritual course.

Yet, there is another kind of ambition; a worldly and sinful one, what is it?

Sinful ambition:

It is an ambition which concentrates on the self and has worldly aims through means that might be wrong.

Examples of this kind of ambition are wealth, sensual delight, lust, money, titles, greatness, vain glory and the like...

The example is the rich fool:

"The land of that rich man yielded plentifully so he said to himself, *"I will pull down my barns and build greater, and there I will store all my crops and my goods. And I will say to my soul, 'Soul, you have many goods laid up for many years; take your ease; eat, drink, and be merry"* (Luke 12:18,19).

Thus he concentrated on material matters and on himself, he did involve God in his ambitions. So he heard God's judgment, *"You fool! This night your soul will be required of you, then whose will those things be which you have provided?"* (Luke 12:20).

Example of King Solomon (the wise):

He had ambitions of greatness and luxury, of sensual pleasure and women. So he said to himself, *"I made my works great, I built myself houses, and planted myself vineyards. I made myself gardens and orchards... I acquired male and female servants... I also gathered for myself silver and gold and the special treasures of Kings and provinces. I acquired male and female singers, the delights of the sons of men... So I became great and excelled more than all who were before me in Jerusalem. Whatever my eyes desired I did not keep from them"* (Eccl. 2:4-10).

But what did Solomon attain from all these ambitions? He said, *"Then I looked on all the works that my hands had done and on the labour in which I toiled; and indeed all was vanity and grasping of the wind. There was no profit under the sun"* (Eccl. 2:11).

Such is the vain worldly ambition; it led Solomon to sin and be under God's punishment. The divine inspiration said about this, *"his wives turned his heart after other gods, and his heart was not loyal to the Lord his God"* (1 Kin. 11:4).

Another example of worldly ambitions is that of those who built the Tower of Babel.

They sought greatness saying, *"Come, let us build ourselves a city, and a tower whose top is in the heavens;*

let us make a name for ourselves... " (Gen. 11:4). Therefore God confused their language and scattered them abroad over the face of all the earth (Gen. 11:7,8).

God disapproved such ambition which was mixed with love for greatness and arrogance...

But the worst ambition indeed was that of Satan!!

He was an angel, even an archangel and was called by the Holy Bible "the anointed cherub who covers", and was perfect in his ways from the day he was created (Ezek. 28:14,15)...

Yet, in spite of his fall, Satan continued in his evil ambitions.

He even dared to say to the Lord Christ - glory be to Him - on the Mount of temptation, *"All these things I will give You if You will fall down and worship me"* (Matt.4:8,9). So, the Lord rebuked him and said, *"Away with you, Satan!"*

However he continued with his ambitions, wishing to compete with God, and to deceive the nations which are in the four corners of the earth (Rev. 20:8), and cause the great apostasy preceding the Second Coming (2 Thess. 2:3,9).

With the same sinful ambition, he made our forefathers fall in the temptation of eating the fruit of the tree of knowledge of good and evil, saying to them, *"you will be like God, knowing good and evil"* (Gen. 3:5).

Some kinds of ambition are associated with conceit.

Conceit may be preceding or succeeding ambition. Preceding conceit is the case of the person who thinks of himself more highly than he ought to think (Rom. 12:3).

Such a person might jump to spiritual levels surpassing his power and thus descends instead of being steadfast in such levels. He might also aspire to have responsibilities beyond his capabilities and thus he fails.

If such a person succeeds in anything, he will become conceited for other things and seek more and more.

Many political leaders failed due to over ambition for continuous triumph, such as Hitler and Napoleon.

The lust for glorification often caused trouble to the ambitious.

It even led them to covetousness and dissatisfaction as Solomon the Wise said, *"All the rivers run into the sea, yet the sea is not full"* (Eccl. 1:7), and also, "The eye is not satisfied with seeing, nor the ear filled with hearing". For this reason, many who seek worldly ambition are in strife, in spite of whatever they gain or achieve.

Difference between the two kinds of ambition :

Sinful ambition: whenever it attains some level, it is puffed up and becomes arrogant. Whereas spiritual ambition rejoices in the Lord in humbleness.

Both kinds of ambition can be apparent in religious life. A person having sinful ambition likes to attain the gifts of the Spirit to be glorified by people, whereas a person having spiritual ambition strives to attain the fruits of the Spirit (Gal. 5:22,23), through which he can enjoy God's love and hidden virtues. Such a person who struggles in the spiritual path, does not take pride in what he attains, but finds spiritual pleasure in his attachment to the Lord. The more he attains, the more he becomes humble, knowing that the way of perfection is still far away. He looks at the lives of the saints and finds that he is no comparison! Whenever he attains something, he remembers the words of the Lord, *"When you have done all those things which you are commanded, say, 'We are unprofitable servants"* (Luke 17:10).

Therefore, many saints who attained very high levels continued to weep for their sins, because in their spiritual ambition they saw higher and higher levels they have not yet attained.

Spiritual people differ from worldly people in regard to the measures of ambition.

✥ A person who has worldly ambition likes for example to become more wealthy and to increase his money day after day and may become greedy. But the ambition of the spiritual person is in giving out his money to the poor to have treasure in heaven.

✥ A person who has worldly ambition likes to be always the first if not the only. He likes the front seats, whereas a spiritual person finds ambition in acquiring the virtue of humility and takes the last seat. He puts before him the words of the Apostle, "...in honour giving preference to one another" (Rom. 12:10), and thus he tries to be last of all and servant of all (Mark 9:35).

Such a person turns into a servant, who loves to serve others and grows in his service, so all people love him for serving them.

A worldly ambitious person competes with people to take their place.

But a spiritually ambitious person helps others to attain what he attained. He does not rival people in the course of life, but with all his heart he wants to attain to God.

Unlike this type, the worldly ambitious person likes to surpass others or detain someone else to beat him.

When Joshua son of Nun saw two men prophesying, he wanted to forbid them - seeing that prophesying should be confined to his master Moses - Moses rebuked him, saying, *"Are you zealous for my sake? Oh, that all the Lord's people were prophets and that the Lord would put His spirit upon them!"* (Num. 11:26-29).

A person who has spiritual ambition, wants to attain the utmost of spirituality due to his love to God, never thinks of rivaling or competing with others or even surpassing them in spirituality.

The ambitious who wants to be superior is overcomed by the self.

God's grace is ready to help everyone achieve their goals. Why then is there competing and rivaling in the way of ambition since there is room for all ?

Or do you want - with this ambition - to win over others in spirituality? And for what reason? Can you find through this victory the spirit of love which your ambition seeks?

The ambition of a person who does not only want to be the first but even to be the only one, is undoubtedly evil ambition.

Such ambitious persons do not like the benefit of others, and this is evil. Ambition like this has deviated and turned to self-love or to selfishness.

Spiritual ambition seeks to rise above certain levels not certain people.

You may rise above certain persons but your spiritual level remains as it is, besides, the desire of surpassing others might lead you to fall into the sin of envy and jealousy which contradicts the spirit of true love. It makes you watch the person who competes with you and you may rejoice for his failure to get an opportunity to surpass him, and thus you lose the purity of heart.

Seek then not to promote yourself in order to conquer over others, and if you do not come first, see that you do not envy him who becomes first but rather rejoice for him.

This is spiritual ambition; to overcome oneself not others.

Let the objective of your seeking perfection be to please God, not to acquire vain glory.

It is a divine commandment that you be perfect (Matt. 5:48), and if you attain this, you ought to rejoice that you will have pleased God by carrying out His commandment. Let this rejoicing be without pride and without comparing yourself to others.

A spiritually ambitious person develops continually.

That is because development is a practical quality for ambition. However in development, a spiritually ambitious person rejoices to see others develop as well. Spiritual ambition seeks spiritual growth in prayers, contemplations, knowing God, love of God, serving Him and love of others; all of which are not fields for competition.

In prayer, a spiritually ambitious person likes to develop and grow whether with regard to the time he spends with God or to the fervency, depth, contemplation, love and faith in his prayers. The same can be said with respect to other virtues; he advances steadily.

Unlike this is the person who has no ambition, who might stop at a certain position and achieve no progress, and this might perhaps lead him to become slack.

In practical life, a person ought to be ambitious.

He should put before him as a goal to succeed in whatever he does as it was said about Joseph the Righteous that he was a successful man, the Lord was with him and made all he did to prosper in his hand. (Gen. 39:2,3).

Someone may ask at this point: Does ambition contradict contentment? No.

Contentment concerns material matters, while ambition concerns spiritual matters.

Both go together and strengthen each other. Some may ask how can ambition attain perfection while perfection is an attribute of God alone. I reply that what is required from a person is relative, not absolute, perfection. If you cannot attain perfection, you should at least grow so that God might see you progressing every day.

Be like the tree which grows every day; for the righteous shall flourish like a palm tree (Ps. 92:12). Do not let your ambition in your work hinder your ambition in your spiritual life.

CHAPTER FIVE

THE CONCEPT OF SIN

Many say 'I have sinned' Very simply!

They do not recognize the significance of the words nor their depth.

We also repeat the same words in the Lord's Prayer, saying, "Forgive us our sins", and in Psalm 51:4, *"Against You, You only, have I sinned, And done this evil in Your sight"*.

We say the same in the Trisagion, "Forgive us our sins, our iniquities and our trespasses". We say these words simply without recognizing their serious significance! So, let us know what is sin?

Sin is against God:

The seriousness of sin lies in its being against God.

Therefore David said to the Lord in the Psalm of repentance, *"Against You, You only, have I sinned, And done this evil in Your sight"*.(Ps 51:4). And about sinners David said they, "have not set You before them", that is: they did not think that You see and hear and watch them. A sinner is like one losing consciousness not knowing what he is doing. He needs someone to awaken him, to make him come to his senses and show him what he is doing.

Sin signifies that you do not feel God's presence.

If you do feel God's presence, you would not commit sin in His eyes without being ashamed! Perhaps this was what occupied the mind of Joseph the Righteous when he said, "How then can I do this great wickedness and sin against God?"

So, when you sin, you sin against God before anything else, you resist Him, disobey Him and defy Him. You grieve His Holy Spirit and defile His dwelling in your heart...

Do you feel all this when you sin or when you confess your sins? Or you just mention your sin simply without feeling its seriousness and offensiveness. It is like a sick person who when asked about his illness replies, 'Oh it is nothing really!' when it may in fact be cancer or AIDS !!

Sin is lawlessness (1 John 3:4). It is transgression and breaking God's commandments, it is lack of concern, and a breach of God's rights, dignity and fatherhood. Sin has thus two aspects: with regard to God, and with regard to people.

With regard to God, sin is revolt against Him.

It is a revolt and disobedience against God. Imagine then that dust and ashes rebel and revolt against God the Creator of heaven and earth!

It is a kind of arrogance that dust revolts against God.

Before breaking the Commandment, arrogance would have broken the heart within.

Sin, thus, is arrogance and haughtiness. Right then are the words said in the book of Proverbs, *"Pride goes before destruction, and a haughty spirit before a fall"* (Prov. 16:18).

Through such pride and arrogance man falls. A humble person who lays himself down to the dust would not fall, but the haughty rises up then falls.

Sin is also lack of love to God.

In this regard, St. John the Apostle says, *"If anyone loves the world, the love of the Father is not in him"* (1 John 2:15).

Two ways then are before a person : either the love of the world or the love of God. And clearly a sinner prefers the love of the world to the love of God; or rather he loves himself more than he loves God (and of course he loves himself in a way that leads it to perdition).

On the other hand sin is lack of love to God, since a sinner disobeys God and revolts against Him.

Sin is enmity with God or disagreement with Him.

This is evident in the words of St. James the Apostle, *"Do you not know that friendship with the world is enmity with God"* (James 4:4).

If the world "enmity" is hard, let us use at least the word "disagreement" as sinners need actually a reconciliation. That is why St. Paul the Apostle said that God *"has given us the ministry of reconciliation"*, so he said, *"we are ambassadors for Christ... we implore you... be reconciled to God"* (2 Cor. 5:19,20).

If you are a sinner, surely you need to be reconciled to God.

Being in disagreement, sin is separation from God.

For, *"what communion has light with darkness?"* (2 Cor.6:14). God is light and sinners live in the outer darkness as they love darkness more than light because their deeds are evil, *"For everyone practicing evil hates the light and does not come to the light, lest his deeds should be exposed"* (John 3:19,20).

When the lost son loved sin, he left his father's house and journeyed to a far country (Luke 15:13), Likewise a sinner is separated from God by his heart, his mind and his deeds. Of such separation the Lord says, *"... but their heart is far from Me"* (Mark 7:6).

Staying in such separation means that the sinner is not concerned or keen to associate with God!! So he stops communing with God and puts an end to his relation with Him and his communion with the Holy Spirit as long as he lives in sin.

By sin we grieve God's Holy Spirit (Eph. 4:30).

This is the case of sin from the beginning as we see in the story of the great flood; for the Holy Bible says, *"the Lord was sorry... and He was grieved in His heart"* (Gen. 6:6).

God is grieved when He sees the creation He made in His image and likeness being destroyed and defiled before His eyes.

When we sin, we do not only grieve God's Spirit, but we also resist and disobey Him as St. Stephen the Deacon said to the Jews on his martyrdom, *"You always resist the Holy Spirit; as your fathers did, so do you"* (Acts 7:51).

A sinner may go to the extent that God's Spirit departs from him.

The Holy Bible said about King Saul, *"But the Spirit of the Lord departed from Saul, and a distressing spirit from the Lord troubled him"* (1 Sam. 16:14). What a hard thing that God's Spirit departs a person!!.

If this is hard for you and you exclaim, 'How can it be that God's Spirit departs from me?', I shall facilitate the meaning for you. I tell you that it is not God's Spirit that departs from you but it is you who departs from God's Spirit. But in both cases there is departing and separation between you and God's Spirit.

St. Paul the Apostle speaks hard words about sin especially about adultery.

He says, *"Do you not know that your bodies are members of Christ? Shall I then take the members of Christ and make them members of a harlot? Certainly not!"* (1 Cor. 6:15).

This means that a person, by sin, defiles God's temple. So the Apostle says, *"Do you not know that you are the temple of God and that the Spirit of God dwells in you? If anyone defiles the temple of God, God will destroy him. For the temple of God is holy, which temple you are"* (1 Cor. 3:16,17).

Therefore, when you say 'I have sinned' think about the words so that you may know what they entail.

Do you realize that they entail the sins we have mentioned before, and the details thereof ? Besides, sin signifies something else :

Sin is a contempt of sonship to God

If you are indeed God's child, created in His image and likeness you will never sin as St. John the Apostle said, *"Whoever has been born of God does not sin... and he cannot sin"*, *"and the wicked one does not touch him"* (1 John 3:9; 1 John 5:18). St. John said also about the Lord, *"If you know that He is righteous, you know that everyone who practices righteousness is born of Him"* (1 John 2:29).

Is a sinner aware, when he is committing sin, that he is God's child and God's image? Or is he at that time surrendering this privilege with its attributes? The Apostle says about this, *"In this the children of God and the children of the devil are manifest"* (1 John 3:10).

Therefore St. Paul rebuked sinners describing them as, *"illegitimate and not sons"* (Heb. 12:8).

Sin is also unfaithfulness to God.

A sinner, by his sinning, is siding with God's enemies, that is, Satan and his hosts, against God and even becoming one of them as the Lord said, rebuking the Jews, *"If you were Abraham's children, you would do the works of Abraham... you are of your father the devil, and the desires of your father you want to do"* (John 8:39,44). St. John the Baptist also reprimanded them, saying, *"Brood of vipers!"* (Matt. 3:7). He meant that they were the children of the devil.

Sin is likewise crucifixion of the Lord Christ.

St. Paul the Apostle says in this regard, *"For it is impossible for those who were once enlightened, and have tasted the heavenly gift... if they fall away to renew them again to repentance, since they crucify again for themselves the Son of God, and put Him to an open shame"* (Heb. 6:4-6).

Or at least, since no sin shall be forgiven unless carried by Christ on the Cross, then, by your sins you are adding a load on Christ's cross and adding bitter drops into the cup He drank.

By your sins you put abominations on Christ's Cross.

He carried the sins of all the world to redeem us by His blood (1 John 2:2), among which are the sins you have committed and still commit.

Hear then in fear what St. Paul the Apostle says, *"Anyone who has rejected Moses' law dies without mercy on the testimony of two or three witnesses. Of how much worse punishment, do you suppose, will be thought worthy who has trampled the Son of God underfoot, counted the blood of the covenant by which he was sanctified a common thing, and insulted the Spirit of grace?"* (Heb. 10:28,29).

Consider these words to recognize how offensive sin is:

Trampled the Son of God underfoot... Counted the blood of the covenant... Insulted the Spirit of grace... Crucify again the Son of God and put Him to open shame. It is indeed unfaithfulness to God and unfaithfulness to the grace we acquired in baptism, for the Apostle says, *"For as many of you as were baptized into Christ have put on Christ"* (Gal. 3:27).

Or do you think that it was Judas alone who betrayed Christ? No, everyone who sins betrays Christ, betrays his own baptism and holy confirmation, and betrays the holy blood which cleanses us from all sin (1 John 1:7).

Sin with regard to man:

Sin with regard to man sin is losing the divine image...

We are created in God's image and likeness, and even though we lost that image when our forefathers fell, we restored it by the grace of the New Testament. However, we lose it again every time we sin because a sinner cannot be in God's image, for God is holy.

Sin is also depriving oneself of God...

You are a branch in the vine as long as you abide in it and as long as the juice of the vine runs in you and you live and give fruit, God prunes you to give more fruit. But the branch which is detached from the vine because of living in sin, will be cast out, and thrown into the fire (John 15:1-6).

When committing sin, you are subjected to the fearful words said by the Lord to those who practice lawlessness, *"I never knew you; depart from Me"* (Matt. 7:23).

It is amazing that these words referred to people who had said to Him, "Lord, have we not prophesied in Your name, cast out demons in Your name, and done many wonders in Your name?"

What a painful thing that the Lord declares that He does not know us!!

The same words were said by the Lord to the foolish *virgins,* "Assuredly, I say to you, I do not know you" (Matt. 25:12). He even shut the door and left them outside, while the wise virgins attended the wedding.

Sin is corruption of the human nature...

You can imagine the condition of Adam and Eve before the fall. They were in wonderful innocence, simplicity and purity. But sin changed their heart and sight, *"the woman saw that the tree was good for food, that it was pleasant to the eyes, and a tree desirable"* (Gen. 3:6).

The tree always existed in the garden, and Eve never looked at it so desirably, yet sin changed the way she perceived the tree; and planted lust in her heart and corrupted her innocent nature.

Man entered into the dualism of good and evil and knowing what is permissible and what is forbidden. He lost his simplicity, knew the lust of the flesh, the lust of the eyes and the pride of life (1 John 2:16). Flesh began to lust against the spirit and the spirit against the flesh and both contradict one another (Gal. 5:1-7).

Believe me, even the features of the face change by sin...

The look, the smile, the tone of the voice and the whole form of the person change. That is why the Apostle advises us, saying, *"be transformed by the renewing of your mind"* (Rom. 12:2).

If you meet one of your friends whom you have not seen for a long time, and this friend has been living in sin, you might say to yourself upon seeing him, "This is not the person I knew before. Everything about him has changed, even his features!"

Sin is defeat, failure and weakness...

This is a fact even though a sinner thinks that he has attained many things from the world, in reality, he has failed. King Saul was not powerful when he chased

David in the wilderness but rather was defeated by himself and his jealousy. Finally he felt his defeat and lifted up his voice and wept, saying to David, *"You are more righteous than I; for you have rewarded me with good, whereas I have rewarded you with evil"* (1 Sam. 24:16,17).

A sinner is a weak person who fails to resist sin and is conquered by evil. He is defeated by his lust for sin. He has become unworthy of God's promises to those who conquer as mentioned in the Lord's messages to the seven churches (Rev. 2:3).

Such a person is defeated, not only by sin that fights from the outside, but more so by the sin that abides within his heart.

Lastly, sin is death...

I cannot find a more wonderful description than that mentioned by the Lord to the angel of the church in Sardis, *"you have a name that you are alive, but you are dead"* (Rev. 1:3). The Lord said the same about the lost son who repented, *"For this my son was dead and is alive again; he was lost and is found"* (Luke 15:24).

CHAPTER SIX

THE CONCEPT OF LOVE & FRIENDSHIP

Love is due to God in the first place:

If we want to understand love according to its true basis, biblically, we should put before us the following fact:

Love is addressed, before anything else, to God - blessed be His name.

This reflects God's words in Deuteronomy, *"You shall love the Lord your God with all your heart, with all your soul, and with all your might"* (Deut. 6:5).

Since this love is with all the heart, where can other kinds of love be? What can we give since all the heart is for God? The only solution is:

Our love for everyone and for everything should be through or within the scope of our love for God.

All the heart is given to God and within this love of God, we love everyone. Therefore the Lord said, *"...and the second is like it; You shall love your neighbor as yourself"* (Matt. 22:39).

But why did He say "like it"? Because it is within the love of God, part of it and not separated from it.

Any love outside the scope of God's love, is wrong.

What then if such love exceeds our love for God? The Lord says in this regard, *"He who loves father or mother more than Me is not worthy of Me. And he who loves son or daughter more than Me is not worthy of Me"* (Matt. 10:37).

The love that exceeds the love of God is for some person or thing other than God Himself. We can say about this :

It is a false love which contradicts God's love and is stronger in the heart than the love for God.

The heart becomes disowned by God, and this false love intrudes God's domain.

Kinds of love:

There is natural love such as love between children and parents. Therefore God likened His love for us to the love of the father for his children.

There is also acquired love such as the love for friends, relatives and colleagues or the love between two engaged persons, or between the husband and wife.

Love might develop gradually.

It may begin as an acquaintance, then develop into friendship. Acquaintance is a relation between two or more persons who may work together or have similar interests, and this may develop into a friendship.

There might be a kind of admiration in some relationships...

However, admiration is something different from love. You may admire an athlete but this does not mean that you love him. When you admire a writer, you admire his thoughts without having any relation with him. There may also arise a mental relation between you and him, but all this is not love. Even though such relations develop into a kind of love, it will be love for his thoughts or style not for his person.

Love is an encounter between two hearts, or a union between two hearts with the same feelings and emotions. In order that such love be holy, the feeling sought should be within God's love, not contradicting or exceeding it.

One of the problems is the case of one sided love.

This means that something is wrong or there is no agreement; for love is supposed to bring forth love.

Love should be reasonable, wise and spiritual; for there

are different kinds of love that may cause harm. True love should be chaste; for there is a difference between love and lust.

I remember that I was once asked to distinguished between them, and I said: **'Love always wants to give, whereas lust always wants to take.'**

Lust, wishing always to take, is characterized by selfishness. It may ruin the other party though it pretends to love. It may confine the other party to it and shut him off from others. It may turn sometimes to a destroying jealousy! In fact, it is not true love; for true love is characterized with giving and sacrifice, even self sacrifice.

Look, then, at yourself in your relation with the other sex and see whether it is a relation of love or lust!

When a young man goes after a girl and destroys her reputation or robs her chastity, what can we call it: love or lust? If he really loves her he would protect her, feel concerned about her reputation as he does for his sister. He would protect her chastity and respect her feelings. He would not let her be infatuated with him and attached to him, then desert her, leaving her confused. Can we call this love?

Some people may call it mere amusement in the life of the young!!!

But what is the cost of such amusement from the spiritual and social aspects? Such amusement occupies the mind and may destroy one's career or hinder the young person's success in study. There is no love whatsoever involved here. What kind of amusement can this be in which chastity and reputation are lost and even the spirituality of both are lost?

True love should be accompanied with purity of heart.

Love between two young people should not abolish their love for God.

The Lord said, *"He who loves father or mother... son or daughter more than Me is not worthy of Me"* (Matt. 10:3,7).

So, is it right for a young man to love a young woman more than God, or for a young woman to love a young man more than God? Is it right that such love involves feelings contradicting with the purity of heart ?

A person who loves you truly never makes you lose your spirituality.

Who loves you truly does not rob for himself your love for God nor decreases its value nor shakes the love of God in your heart. He cannot leave you in conflict between two kinds of love: a spiritual love and the love of the flesh, or love for God and love for a human being.

Love is not self enjoyment at the expense of another person!

It is rather a self-denial and a self sacrifice as Jonathan did for the sake of his friend David; exposing himself to the anger of his father by defending David.

The best example of love is the sacrifice on the cross for our sake as the Lord said, *"For God so loved the world that He gave His Only Begotten Son... "* (John 3:16).

What then can we say about love which leads to marriage?

The important thing is: How can we be sure that it leads to marriage? What are the limitations of such love or such relation which is called love leading to marriage? Is it love between two engaged persons as a condition? Or is it love without any legal relation? What is its end? And what can protect it from deviation?

True love is everlasting love.

It continues and never fails (1Cor. 13:8), if the couple love each other strongly and wish that such love continues between them throughout their life on earth. This love will also continue with them in eternity. This cannot be realized unless their love is chaste so that they may enter Paradise together, then enter together into the

Kingdom in eternity. But if one of them perishes on the way, they will not be together in the kingdom of heaven.

They should support each other on the spiritual way.

Suppose they lived together in sin, then one of them repented and the other did not. They will be separated after death; one will go to Paradise, and the other to Hades. They will never meet in the eternal life and thus their love is not everlasting. Perpetual love is spiritual.

Love has various kinds of domains.

There is love among family members - parents and children, brothers and sisters, and husband and wife. All these kinds of love and relationships are approved by the Holy Bible and by nature.

Friendship:

There is the love of friends such as the love between David and Jonathan of which David said after the death of Jonathan, *"I am distressed for you my brother Jonathan; you have been very pleasant to me, your love to me was wonderful, surpassing the love of women"* (2 Sam. 1:26).

It was pure love between two spirits.

On the other hand, love which has a physical relation such as that between husband and wife, is not permitted by the Holy Bible outside wedlock.

At this point we move to friendship: what is its concept? And what are its limits?

Friendship is a feeling of amiability which might be between one man and another, one woman and another, or among the members of one family or between two families with their members whether men or women. It might be between two sexes within the scope of spiritual love without any physical feeling. A friend should be true in friendship. He should be righteous so as to lead his friend to goodness.

A friend who defends you when you do wrong and encourages you to continue is not a true friend.

Whoever does this is not your true friend. His love to you is harmful. So you should choose your friends by those who participate with you in righteousness and who do not flatter you at the expense of truth nor encourage you to do wrong.

Wrong love:

There are different kinds of wrong love:

Love may be wrong in itself or in its means, its course or outcome.

An example of wrong means is the love Rebecca had for her son Jacob.

She wanted Jacob to have the blessing, but she resorted to wrong means, which was to deceive his father. Thus she exposed him to God's punishment, which was followed by the deceit of Laban when he gave Leah to marry instead of Rachel and when he changed his wages. Jacob was also deceived by his own sons who pretended that a wild beast devoured his son Joseph and he lived all his life in turmoil.

Rebecca was also wrong in that her love was not complete. She did not love Esau as she loved Jacob. Jacob also, when he grew old, did not love all his children in the same degree. He loved Joseph more than the others and this made them jealous and sought to injure him.

The Lord wants us to love all people, even enemies and those who offend us. It is also written, *"If your enemy hungers, feed him; if he thirsts, give him a drink"* (Rom. 12:20).

Whoever loves at the expense of others, has no love in his heart.

An example of this is Jezebel who loved her husband King Ahab and helped him to take the vineyard of Naboth. She devised a plan to accuse Naboth by false witnesses and put him to death. Thus her love for her husband was wrong love that led him to oppress and kill and to deserve the Lord's revenge (1 Kin. 21)

Love might be wrong with regard to its outcome.

An example is that of the women who admired David's victory over Goliath and sang to him saying *"Saul has slain his thousands, and David his ten thousands."*(1Sam. 18:7). Thus they implanted jealousy in Saul's heart that led him to maltreat David bitterly and seek to kill him.

Another example is of the people who kept shouting to Herod, *"The voice of a god not of a man."*
(Acts 12:22). So, an angel of the Lord struck him, and he was eaten by worms and died because he did not give glory to God.

Another kind of wrong love is encouraging sinners.

An example of this is those who followed heretics throughout history and encouraged them creating a popularity to support their theological mistakes. This made them adhere to their heresies and heterodoxies and thus the church ex-communicated them. They lost their eternity, whereas if those followers had not encouraged them, they would have forsaken their heresies for not finding supporters.

Some of those followers even continued to spread the views of the hereties after their death.

It is not love to encourage a person to continue in sin.

Nor is it love to defend him or support him financially. But true love leads to repentance through revealing one's mistake, reprimanding him for it and calling him to stop doing it.

Love which encourages one to sin is not love, as stated by the Holy Bible , *"He who justifies the wicked, and he who condemns the just,* both of them alike are an abomination to the Lord"* (Prov. 17:15).

A person who justifies the wicked out of love, loses God's love and becomes an abomination to Him. Even this love for the wicked leads him to perish eternally as he is considered taking part in sin and the responsibility for the sinful act, its results and punishment.

When such a person perishes, he who encouraged him will be among the reasons that led to his perdition and at the same time he will be deemed resisting Truth, who is God.

The mother who conceals the mistakes of her son, so that his father may not know and punish him, does not truly love her son but rather does him harm. She corrupts him and destroys his character and his relation with God.

Also the mother who spoils her son is in a way destroying him. So the saying goes, 'Who makes you weep is weeping for you, and who makes you laugh is laughing at you'.

When you love a person, do not defend him in his wrong doing, but save him.

You can lead him to repentance, thus saving him and saving yourself of being condemned with him.

True love is to deliver him of his faults, or to justify his faults before others.

Reprimanding is therefore a kind of love.

Disciplining from those who have authority is an evidence of love as it is said about God- blessed be His name - *"For whom the Lord loves He corrects"* (Prov. 3:12), (Heb. 12:6).

Some people - regretfully - think that punishment is against love!! No, this is wrong; for punishment keeps you from continuing in sin. If a sinner does not benefit from it, the others will benefit as St. Paul the Apostle said to his disciple St. Timothy, *"Those who are sinning rebuke in the presence of all, that the rest also may fear"* (1 Tim. 5:20).

Some people may think that love calls them to support others even in their wrong doings.

An example of this is the student who assists his colleague to cheat in the exams out of love for him! Or the father priest who helps one to conclude an illegal marriage claiming that he is helping a person to marry the one he loves; or the doctor who helps a girl who sinned to abort the child to avoid embarrassment.

Another example of wrong love is the husband who restrains his wife at home.

Restraining is not correct, but a husband should deepen his love for his wife so that she might be attached to him. The wife's love for God prevents her from deceiving her husband. Restraining and restricting the wife at home is a kind of selfishness which deprives her from enjoying her life without any fault on her part.

Over zealous love is also a wrong type of love.

An example of this is the love of Peter the Apostle for the Lord Christ. This love made him draw his sword and strike the high priest's servant, and cut off his right ear. The Lord reprimanded him for that action (John 18:10,11).

Another example of wrong love is the mother who is over protective of her children and their health, even preventing them from fasting. She may even ask his father confessor to prevent him.

Unlike this is the saintly mother who, in the days of martyrdom, witnessed her children being martyred before her eyes, even on her lap, and yet encouraged them in their faith.

When we speak about love, we mean true love which results in one's salvation and success on the spiritual way.

Practical Love:

True love is practical love.

St. John the Apostle said in this regard, *"Let us not love in word or in tongue, but in deed and in truth"* (1 John 3:18).

The parents' love for a child is practical love, for they care for their nourishment, health, cleanliness and education. They are also concerned with their spiritual life; they instruct him in religion and encourage him in virtue.

The Song of Songs says concerning love, *"Set me a seal upon your heart, as a seal upon your arm"* (Song 8:6).

The expression "a seal upon your heart" means your emotions and inner feelings, whereas the expression "a seal upon your arm" means giving hand in work.

St. Peter the Apostle was not a seal upon the heart when he said, *"Even if all are made to stumble, yet I will not be... if I have to die with You, I will not deny You!."* (Mark 14:29,30). And when he denied, he was not a seal upon the arm.

So, a seal upon the heart refers to faith, and a seal upon the arm refers to works. Love for God requires both matters together, and love for people also requires feelings and work; for such is practical love.

With regard to pastors, the Holy Bible says, *"The good shepherd gives His life for the sheep"* (John 10:11). Giving oneself is practical love.

God - the Good Shepherd - as mentioned in the Holy Bible, *"demonstrates His own love toward us, in that while we were still sinners, Christ died for us"* (Rom. 5:8).

It was practical love demonstrated in the Incarnation, Crucifixion and redemption.

Love is an emotion expressing itself in action

The Lord says, *"My son, give Me your heart"* (Prov.23:26). Does this mean that God wants mere emotions? No, for He says immediately after, *"And let your eyes observe My ways."* Here love is required together with action. Thus the Lord says, *"If anyone loves Me, he will keep My word"* (John 14:23), and also, *"If you keep My commandments, you will abide in My love"* (John 15:10).

Love for God is not theoretical love, nor mere emotions.

Your love for God is demonstrated in your obedience to Him and in keeping His commandments. It is revealed also in spreading His kingdom on earth, in serving Him and in serving His church and His children.

But to say that you love God while you are doing nothing, is mere theoretical love which is not acceptable.

Here I remember with great admiration, those who preached God's word in countries where people are cannibals.

This is the sacrificing love; the love of a person who gives people God's word to feed on, even if some of them feed on him!!

The relationship with God:

When we speak about love, we do not only speak about dealings among people but rather more about the relationship with God. When the Lord Christ was talking with the Father about His relationship with His disciples in the famous Chapter of John chapter 17, He said, *"I have given to them the words which You have given Me"*

(John 17:8), *"And I have declared to them Your name and will declare it, that the love with which You loved Me may be in them, and I in them"* (John 17:26).

It is a relationship involving recognition and love as well as sacrifice.

We find an example of this in the words of St. Paul the Apostle about his ministry, *"in journey often, in perils of waters, in perils of robbers, in perils of my own countrymen... in perils in the wilderness, in perils in the sea, in perils among false brethren; in weariness and toil, in sleeplessness often, in hunger and thirst, in fastings often, in cold and nakedness..."* (2 Cor. 11:26,27).

You would ask St. Paul: Is this ministry? And I can imagine him replying: It is rather love.

As for you, is your love for God mere words or action?

Does your love involve sacrifice and giving and the spreading of God's word?

Does your love involve control over your tongue, thoughts and lusts?

Does love appear in your prayers, ministry and forbearance?

Do you say in your prayer with the Psalmist : *"I will lift up my hands in Your name. My soul shall be satisfied as with marrow and fatness"* (Ps. 63:4).

Is your ministry a kind of love as that of the Lord Christ of whom it was said, *"having loved His own who were in the world, He loved them to the end"* (John 13:1).

True love is also without hypocrisy (Rom. 12:9).

This should be the kind of love whether towards God or towards people.

Let not our hearts be different from our tongue and our tongue from our emotions.

CHAPTER SEVEN
THE CONCEPT OF OFFENSE

What is an offense :

The Lord Christ - glory be to Him - said about offenses, *"Woe to the world because of offenses... Woe that man by whom the offense comes!"* (Matt. 18:7), *"But whoever causes one of these little ones who believe in Me to sin, it would be better for him if millstone were hung around his neck, and he drowned in the depth of the sea"* . (Matt. 18:6).

If offense is so serious in the punishment it entails, what is an offense?

An offense causes a person to fall.

An offense may be intentional when it causes another to fall. The punishment in this case is more serious than that in the case of unintentional offense.

The first offense in man's history was introduced through the devil.

He caused our first parents to fall; for they were simple, knowing no evil and he intended on making them fall through deceit and temptation. By this offense, death entered into the world and the devil caused the corruption of human nature.

Offense comes through various means: when a person causes offense to another through making him familiar with sin, facilitating sin to him, letting him taste sin or introducing it under a false concept, such as giving it the name of a virtue or telling him about the benefits and advantages of sin!!

Knowledge of sin:

This means that a person is aware of the things which harm him spiritually.

Thus knowledge which defiles his thoughts is introduced into his mind.

This knowledge may arouse lusts within and make him fall into sin. Perhaps this was in the mind of Solomon the Wise when he said, *"For in much wisdom is much grief, and he who increases knowledge increases sorrow"* (Eccl. 1:18).

Eve fell through the knowledge that came to her which was false; for the devil lied when he said to her, *"your eyes will be opened, and you will be like God... "* (Gen. 3:5). However these words changed Eve's sight, thought and emotion: *"So when the woman saw that the tree was good for food, that it was pleasant to the eyes, and a tree desirable to make one wise, she took of its fruit and ate..."* (Gen. 3:6).

So a person who encourages a friend with harmful information, is offending him.

Such is the case, for example, of a person who gives his friend information falsely about another person, condemning him, or introduces some ideas that may corrupt him morally, or suspicions which may shake his faith. The friend after such meeting will say, 'Oh I wish I had not met him or heard what he had to say!'

Another example is the evil environment and the thoughts introduced in it.

About this the Apostle said, *"Evil company corrupts good habits"* (1 Cor. 15:33).

Thus, with the offense on one side and the bad example on the other side, a person becomes aware of deceit. For example, the pupil who learns to miss school or to cheat in exams, or children and youth who become involved in gangs for the purpose of learning how to pick pockets, or some youth who gather together and teach a new friend drug addiction or gambling, all these are stumbling blocks, and the Psalmist said concerning this : *"Blessed is the man who walks not in the counsel of the ungodly, nor stands in the path of sinners, nor sits in the seat of the scornful"* (Ps. 1:1).

A stumbling block also is the person who introduces to you to a wrong thought without refuting it.

He may introduce to you all evidences of the wrong thought and stop at this point without commenting on it or giving refutations destroying that thought. And when he is attacked for what he said, he replies. 'I did not say that these are my views, but I just mentioned them for information!'

Such people may have followers, disciples and lovers who repeat and teach the same ideas and they become stumbling blocks.

Evading such a person is chastity not contention

Evading them is avoidance of causes of offenses and avoidance of knowledge of offense; for a person who causes offense leads his friend to lose the simplicity and innocence he had before. It seems as if he is saying to his friend the same words which the devil said to Eve, "your eyes will be opened". The eyes become open to know sin.

Facilitating sin:

It is another kind of offense; for it is probable that a person knows sin but does not practice it as long as the door is closed before him. So, whoever facilitates the matter to him is offending him, as for example when a person makes another familiar with places and means of sin leading him to those places, removing fear from his heart and removing obstacles from his way.

An example is the behaviour of Jezebel by which she facilitated King Ahab to take possession of the vineyard of Naboth the Jesreelite (1 Kin. 21), and also the purpose of Ahithophel's counsel to Absalom to enable him strike his father David (2 Sam. 17).

All this is more serious and dangerous than mere knowledge of sin; for remedy of sin is much easier than remedy of the taste of sin.

Tasting sin:

It is the first practical step towards committing sin, such as when a person offers a cigarette to someone to smoke, or a rose containing heroin to smell; or lets him win in gambling to continue playing; or gives him a glass of wine to taste; or opens for him the door to practice the sins of youth.

Giving another name to sin:

It is an offense to give sin the name of a virtue, or another acceptable name.

For example, when a person spreads some heresy, he says that it is the right concept of religion. The person who teaches his friend gambling calls it a kind of amusement or entertainment. The person who causes another to commit adultery, says that this is a cure for repression and its harmful effects. The person who assists someone to evade taxes, says that this is mere avoidance of the exaggeration and oppression of the tax-assessing commissions... etc. The devil - in the offense - does not fight openly.

Kinds of offenses:

Not all offenses are in the field of youth sins as some may think.

There are offenses in the field of religion as in the case of heretics and those who spread suspicions concerning religion or spread atheism or deny the resurrection and miracles of Christ.

There are also offenses in the field of philosophy and ideology where principles and values are shaken. This is the case of the heretics who introduce new ideas to destroy the established ideas under the name of science and innovation.

The Arians were more dangerous than Arius himself and they offended Athanasius more. So, it is well said by St. James the Apostle, *"My brethren, let not many of you become teachers, knowing that we shall receive a stricter judgment"* (James 3:1).

But, what is the reason? *"For we all stumble in many things".* It is the stumbling block of teaching, when one stumbles by himself, seeing himself right, wise in his own eyes (Prov. 3:7).

Moreover he makes others stumble through spreading his wrong teaching.

Do not, then, accept every new thought that destroys what you have previously received.

Such thoughts may be a stumbling block for you, for some would try to present something new by abolishing old traditions to prove themselves more knowledgeable .

Some of those work in Biblical criticism. They are clergymen and professors of Theology in foreign universities. However they are stumbling blocks and according to the words of the Apostle "they shall receive a stricter judgment," being condemned for their errors and for spreading such errors.

Bad Example:

This is an offense; for others fall in errors due to imitating those examples, who - whether being leaders or colleagues - do not intend to make others fall, but they become a cause. Others may learn from their routine, coming late to work, justifying errors, mistreating the public and delaying their work, low production, writing false or forged reports ... etc.

A person absorbs from society many things. He may absorb habits and offenses.

In this regard, we see parents and the influence on their children; for children see their fathers and mothers examples to be followed.

A stumbling block for the simple who have no discernment are those who are more experienced, more knowledgeable or higher in rank; for the simple stumble not because they criticize them but they imitate them.

Employees of low rank, when being promoted, may follow the example of his precedent and thus stumble.

Culture and the Mass Media:

All audio visual media might be a stumbling block, if the programs presented are offensive to the audience; for they will have their impact on the personality, whether on thinking or behaviour or on the interior feelings and emotions.

Likewise, all sources of thought, whether books, magazines, newspapers, pamphlets, leaflets etc... These might be a stumbling block if they have a bad effect on people's thoughts, feelings and behaviour and lead them onto a path which is harmful to them and to the community.

Someone once said: 'Tell me what you read, and I'll tell you who you are.'

To these words I add; the matter is not confined only to what you read, but it extends also to what you see and what you hear. Cassettes, television and video may have a dangerous effect on people, as well as cinema films and plays, most of which may be a stumbling block.

We should then be careful regarding all this whether with respect to ourselves or our children.

The adults and the young:

A adult should be very careful in his words and behaviour lest he should offend the young or the weak, as the Apostle says, *"But beware lest you become a stumbling block to those who are weak"* (1 Cor. 8:9). And he repeats, *"the weak brother... for whom Christ died..."* (1 Cor. 8:11), and says also, *"Therefore, if food makes my brother stumble, I will never again eat meat, lest I make my brother stumble"* (1 Cor. 8:13). The Apostle says concerning conscience, *"Conscience, I say, not your own, but that of the other... not seeking my own profit, but the profit of many, that they may be saved"* (1Cor. 10:29-33).

The Lord Christ spoke about offenses and warned against offending the young, saying, *"But whoever causes one of these little ones who believe in Me to sin... Woe to that man by whom the offense comes!"* (Matt. 18:6,7).

The strong may be able to resist the causes of offense, but what about the weak?

By the strong we mean the person who is spiritually strong, who has self control and maturity. Such a strong person can discern what is wrong and can resist it. However, he may fall in condemning its doer. But the problem is that of offending the weak, the young or the simple.

A weak person may say: If the adult falls, what can I, the weak person, do? He may yield or fall out of despair or submission.

A weak person stumbles when he sees the ideals fall before him.

Therefore St. Paul the Apostle reprimanded St. Peter the Apostle before the others, saying, *"If you, being a Jew, live in the manner of Gentiles and not as the Jews, why do you compel Gentiles to live as Jews?"* (Gal. 2:14). St. Paul said this because he found, *"that even Barnabas was carried away with their hypocrisy"* (Gal. 2:13). Barnabas was thus offended by them.

Adults should hence be careful in their behaviour; by this I mean the parents in the family, the teachers towards the pupils, the ministers towards those whom they serve, the priests towards the congregation and the guides towards those who seek their counsel.

They ought not be a stumbling block with their conversation, behaviour, movement and features.

They should be keen about keeping order, obeying the law and keeping the commandments. When deacons, for example, are careful not to talk during prayer, and are careful to respect the altar and the prayers, they can be an example to the congregation. Likewise when they behave in a wrong way, they will be an offense to the congregation who may follow their example.

The person who talks in church during prayers commits many faults:

First : Not respecting the church, not respecting the prayers, and lack of God's fear in their heart.

Second : He becomes an offense to others, who will either imitate him, or commit the sin of condemning him.

The same may be said about a person who keeps looking at his watch during a meeting or a sermon, or who leaves church before the final blessing or dismissal.

A person should avoid being a stumbling block, even if his behaviour is not wrong.

When the Lord Christ was asked to pay tax, knowing that tax was only to be taken from strangers, said to Peter, *"Nevertheless, lest we offend them, go to the sea, cast in a hook and take the fish... you will find a piece of money; take that and give it to them for Me and you"* (Matt. 17:27).

In order not to offend them also, He went to be baptized by John the Baptist to set the example for repentance, though He needed no repentance.

The Lord Christ obeyed the law in many things which were not necessary for Him, and St. Mary also did the same so that they might not be an offense to others.

Conscience:

Some have a strict conscience that doubts everything and thinks that right is wrong, and others have free conscience that justifies many actions.

Conscience also has a relation to offense, as the following examples will show:

Is beauty, for example, a stumbling block?

Suppose there is a beautiful girl: some look at her and lust for her. Is she considered a stumbling block for them? And if so, what is her guilt?

She is not a stumbling block. The stumbling block is in the hearts of those who lust for her. It is their fault not hers. Take for example St. Justina who was very pretty and when someone lusted for her he resorted to magic to be able to have her. Was that saint an offense to him? No, but the offense was in the heart of that impure man.

And what do you say about the two angels whom the people of Sodom lusted for?

Were the two angels a cause of offense? God forbid. It was the fault of those deviant people. Therefore, the two angels struck them with blindness as a punishment for their impure lust (Gen. 19:4-11).

The scribes and Pharisees criticized the Lord Christ because He worked miracles on the Sabbath. Was the Lord Christ an offense to them? God forbid. It was lack of understanding on their part a lack of purity in their hearts.

The offense came from within them.

Many saints were accused unjustly by people, such as St. Macarius the Great, St. Marina, and St. Aphram the

Syrian. These saints were not stumbling blocks and so God revealed their innocence. Hence, let us contemplate on the words of the Apostle, *"To the pure all things are pure"* (Titus 1:15). The impure are offended by many things, for they think in an impure way, whereas the pure think with purity and so they are not offended by the things that offend others.

Only a pure conscience can judge justly on these matters.

The Lord commanded us to conceal our virtues. But if we conceal our prayers, our fasting and our almsgiving according to the Lord's command (Matthew 6), will this offend people in that they will think we do not pray or fast? Or should we reveal our virtues in order not to offend them even though we break the Lord's commandment by this? It is a matter of conscience.

The important thing is that we do not provide a cause for offense.

In this case if someone is offended because of us - though we do not mean it - it will be his guilt.

Can we say that David the Prophet was an offense to King Saul, when he defeated Goliath?

Undoubtedly not. David could not have left Goliath defy the armies of the Lord, and he attributed the victory to the Lord, saying to Goliath, *"This day the*

Lord will deliver you into my hand, for the battle is the Lord's, and He will give you into our hands"
(1 Sam.17:46,47).

What offended Saul was the jealousy in his heart when the women sang, *"Saul has slain his thousands, and David his ten thousands"* (1 Sam.18:7).

David the Prophet said also in the Psalm: *"Those who hate me without a cause, Are more than the hairs of my head"* (Ps. 69:4).

Had David offended them, so they hated him? No, for he said they hated him without a cause. The cause was malice they bare in their hearts, the jealousy of his godliness and victories or their desire to usurp his power as they had done with Absalom.

Hypocrisy:

Some people - in order not to offend - become hypocritical.

They pretend righteousness in order not to offend others by their sins.

They may also pretend fasting so as not to offend people while in fact they are not fasting. In this way, they fall into two sins: breaking the fast and hypocrisy.

One should not feign righteousness to avoid being a cause of offense! The right thing is to behave well and be actually righteous in order not to offend people.

CHAPTER EIGHT

THE CONCEPT OF MEEKNESS

The importance of meekness:

The most beautiful verses on the importance of gentleness or meekness are :

The words of the Lord Christ - glory be to him, *"Learn from Me, for I am gentle and lowly in heart, and you will find rest for your souls"* (Matt. 11:29). All perfection existed in the Lord Christ, yet He concentrated on gentleness in the first place and revealed that it is a cause of rest for the soul.

St. Paul the Apostle introduced gentleness as a fruit of the Spirit (Gal. 5:23).

St. James the Apostle said, *"Who is wise and understanding among you? Let him show by good conduct that his works are done in the meekness of wisdom"* (James 3:13).

In the Beatitudes, the Lord mentioned it at the beginning, *"Blessed are the meek, for they shall inherit the earth"* (Matt. 5:5).

In the Psalms meekness is beatified in many places among which is: *"But the meek shall inherit the earth, And shall delight themselves in the abundance of peace"* (Ps. 37:11).

St. Peter the Apostle, speaking about the adornment of women, said, *"the incorruptible ornament of a gentle and quiet spirit, which is very precious in the sight of God"* (1 Pet. 3:4).

Since gentleness or meekness is of such importance let us inquire:

What is meekness and what are the attributes of the meek?

What is gentleness?

A meek or gentle person is calm, good-natured, lenient, and cheerful. He is calm, does not get angry, agitated, or furious, but their voice is gentle and pleasant. He does not get nervous for he is composed.

The Lord Christ in His meekness was described as, *"He will not quarrel nor cry out, nor will anyone hear His voice in the streets. A bruised reed He will not break, and smoking flax He will not quench"* (Matt. 12:19,20), (Is. 42:2,3).

A meek person is calm internally and externally. Peace dominates his heart, so he does not feel anxious or disturbed. He is on peaceful terms with all, he attacks no one, hurts no one, is not harsh, and is not revengeful, even when attacked.

The meek person never interferes in the affairs of others, nor sets himself a guard over their works. Thus he condemns no one, and even if he interferes in correcting someone, he does it calmly as the Apostle said, *"Brethren, if a man is overtaken in any trespass, you who are spiritual restore such one in a spirit of gentleness, considering yourself lest you also be tempted."* (Gal. 6:1). He restores such a brother by calm persuasion, in humbleness fearing lest he himself be tempted.

A meek person bears others with long-suffering. He is tolerant; he puts before him the words of the Scriptures, *"A soft answer turns away wrath"* (Prov. 15:1).

He looks towards God's example in forbearance and long-sufferance towards sinners.

He never grumbles either in his relation with God or with people, but on the contrary, he is always cheerful and smiling.

The meek person is often shy. He is known for his bashfulness and even as one of the fathers said, 'He does not look fully at anyone's face'. He does not examine one's features nor go deep within them to know their hearts.

He does not analyze people and their feelings for his looks are simple. He is shy and always bashful.

The meek are easy to deal with. He is simple; he has no cunning, craftiness or malice. He is plain; does not conceal things and show others, nor complicate matters. He is clear in his dealings; does not beat around the bush nor makes plans. Dealing with him gives comfort because he is simple, clear and pleasant.

He is gentle, sweet and good-natured. He is loved by all because he is good. Even if he is oppressed by some, many will defend him and rebuke the person who oppressed him, saying, 'Have you found no one but this good person to treat unjustly?' Moreover, the person who treated him unjustly would come eventually and apologize to the person he accused and also those who defended the accused, because he did no harm but showed love and gentleness to all people. Suffice that the Lord says, *"Blessed are the meek, for they shall inherit the earth"* (Matt.5:5). He will inherit the earth and heaven as well, besides having God's grace with him always.

A meek person is obliging. He is inclined to comfort people and not resist them. He does not go on arguing, discussing, persisting and inquiring but does what is good and quietly, immediately without delay and without discussion. He does not hold to his views in every thing as some may do, but lets it pass as long as the matter is not against the commandment. Therefore he is not biased, for he loves all people.

Losing meekness:

A meek person maintains his meekness.

He does not lose his meekness when he holds a high position or enjoys some authority. He maintains his meekness whatever high position he attains. His heart is not elevated by the power of authority.

The meek does not lose his meekness while correcting others. If he is in a position that gives him an authority to correct others, he does it without being harsh or severe and without coarse behaviour or voice.

He does not lose his meekness if he defends what is right. He defends quietly without hurting the feeling of anyone. Even when he speaks frankly, his frankness is not hurting; for he expresses what he wants to say in a gentle way.

At this point we remember the way the Lord Christ talked to the Samaritan woman. He revealed to her everything gently without hurting her feelings (John 4). A truly meek person never loses his meekness under the pretext of being firm or bold or by misusing power and dignity.

A person cannot say that he lost his meekness because he was born with a fiery temper. Moses the Black was of this kind, but he acquired meekness through the life of repentance. He began his life with harshness, but he trained himself until he became a very kind hearted person.

Meekness and courage:

Some people misunderstand meekness, imagining that the meek is a sluggish person with no influence or effectiveness and that meekness is mere slackening!

Those people may ridicule the meek and treat them with disdain. They may mock him because of his tolerance and patience. They think that because the meek do not condemn people, he would do nothing if he saw evil prevailing over good! No. This is not true meekness.

The right concept of meekness recognizes being connected with manliness, self-respect, courage and gallantry.

We usually remember that the meek person is actually a good, lenient and indulgent person and ignore that he has also courage, self respect and gallantry!

The profound words said in the Book of Ecclesiastes, apply to the conduct of the meek in various situations : *"To everything there is a season, a time for every purpose under heaven... a time to keep silence, and a time to speak"* **(Eccl.3:1,7).**

Goodness is the general nature of the meek. However, there is time in his life for courage and time for gallantry, but without violence in any case.

Examples:

The Lord Christ in His meekness and firmness:

The Lord Christ, the great example of whom it was said, *"He will not quarrel or cry out, nor will anyone hear His voice in the streets,"* we see Him firm and strong in cleansing the Temple and driving out those who bought and sold there, saying to them, *"It is written 'My house shall be called a house of prayer, but you have made it a den of thieves'"* (Matt. 21:12,13).

He was also strong and firm in reprimanding the scribes and Pharisees (Matt. 23).

He was firm in explaining the Law of the Sabbath and doing good on that day, though He found resistance.

Moses the prophet:

He was known for his amazing gentleness and humbleness: *"Now the man Moses was very humble, more than all men who were on the face of the earth"* (Num. 12:3).

When Moses came down from the mountain with the two tablets of the Testimony in his hand and saw the people

111

singing and dancing in worship of a golden calf, he was not passive under pretext of humbleness and gentleness but became hot with anger, cast the tablets out of his hands and broke them. Then he took the calf which they made, burnt it in the fire and ground it to powder and scattered it on the water (Ex. 32:19,20). He reprimanded Aaron the high priest who shook before him.

David the Prophet:

Was bold and brave when he saw Goliath defying the armies of the living God, whereas all the army stood in fear in front of that valiant.

The gentle David was the only one who could say, *"who is this uncircumcised Philistine that he should defy the armies of the living God?"* (1 Sam. 17:26).

He inquired from the people about him and was not affected when his elder brother scorned him. Then he said to King Saul, *"Let no man's heart fail because of him... "* (1 Sam. 17:32), and drew near and fought the Philistine without fear and said to him, *"You come to me with a sword, with a spear, and with a javelin. But I come to you in the name of the Lord of hosts... This day the Lord will deliver you into my hand"*. (1 Sam.17:45,46).

This is David, the gentle youth, with the flute and lyre and at the same time the zealous warrior and valiant.

St. Paul the Apostle:

A good natured calm person who when rebuking the Corinthians said to them, *"Now I, Paul, myself am pleading with you by the meekness and gentleness of Christ, who in presence am lowly among you, but being absent am bold toward you"* (2 Cor. 10:1).

And to the Ephesians he said, *"remember that for three years I did not cease to warn everyone night and day with tears"* (Acts 20:31).

In spite of this meekness and gentleness, St. Paul was like a lion in preaching and evangelizing. When he was speaking about righteousness, self-control and the judgment to come, Felix the Governor was afraid and answered him, *"Go away for now; when I have a convenient time I will call for you"* (Acts 24:25).

And when he stood before King Agrippa, the King said to him, *"You almost persuade me to become a Christian" (Acts 26:28).*

In spite of his meekness, St. Paul also did not refrain from rebuking St. Peter the Apostle, and said, *"But when I saw that they were not straight forward about the truth of the gospel, I said to Peter before them all, 'If you, being a Jew, live in the manner of Gentiles and not as the Jews, why do you compel Gentiles to live as Jews?"* (Gal. 2:14).

Elihu, the son of Barachel :

The fourth friend of Job. Because of his meekness he kept silent while Job's three other friends were talking (their speeches taking 28 Chapters of the Book of Job). Elihu did not open his mouth due to his exceeding meekness, seeing that the other three were older than him.

However, he could not keep silent more than this when he found that all the others spoke wrongly. The Scripture says, *"Then the wrath of Elihu, the son of Barachel the Buzite, of the family of Ram, was aroused against Job ... his wrath was aroused because he justified himself rather than God. Also against his three friends his wrath was aroused because they had found no answer, and yet had condemned Job ... and said, 'I am young in years, and your are very old; therefore I was afraid, and dared not declare my opinion to you ..."* (Job 32:2-7). Then he proceeded to rebuke them.

Indeed, there is a time for every purpose under heaven. There is time for the silence of the meek and a time for talk, a time for his gentleness and a time for his firmness.

Remarks:

1. If one of your relatives is about to marry a particular person without receiving permission or the blessing from the church would you keep silent under the pretext of meekness and gentleness, or would you warn your relative concerning the probability of a harmful marriage?

If you keep silent, then this is not meekness, for you ought to warn your relative against this wrong situation and explain to him calmly the reasons why. This is not against meekness as long as you explain the matter without being insulting or hurting. Just say the words of St. John the Baptist, *"It is not lawful for you to have her"* (Mark 6:18).

2.   Or if you see one of your acquaintances about to end a marriage, would you keep silent for the sake of meekness? No. You should say to him this is wrong and God will not bless such a marriage if you end it.

This does not contradict with meekness. You are not asked to become enraged and to shout, but simply just to warn calmly.

3.   God loves Truth, and loves to see us defending it in the right way. He says in the Book of Jeremiah, *"Run to and fro through the streets of Jerusalem; see now and know and seek in her open places if you can find a man, if there is anyone who executes judgment, who seeks the truth, and I will pardon her"* (Jer. 5:1).

Defending truth is a virtue which God requires. If you walk in it you will walk in righteousness, and this is not against meekness as long as you follow the right way.

CHAPTER NINE

THE CONCEPT OF TRUTH & JUSTICE

Truth is fact:

The first concept of Truth is the true fact.

The Lord Christ often started His talk with the words, *"Assuredly, I say to you," "Most assuredly I say to you."* (Matt. 8:10), (John 5:19,24,25), (John 8:34,51,58).

In law courts a witness swears, saying, 'I'll say the truth, all the truth, and nothing but the truth'. There is also an important principle which states, half facts are not facts.

The seriousness of half facts:

It is said that half facts do not fairly present facts.

A woman may complain that her husband has wronged her, however, she neglects to mention how she too has wronged him. Thus, she only considers the situation from one side.

Someone else may say that he was punished by the Church, or dismissed from work but does not mention the reason why.

Thus his words do not give a true presentation of the fact.

This is why investigations are made in lawsuits, for the purpose of ascertaining the true facts.

The fact is complete when the matter is researched from all aspects, opinions presented from both sides, the cause and the consequence examined and the action and the reaction known. When one side is heard, the fact is not clear. Therefore, the investigator needs to confront both parties.

When anyone tells you something, you ought to question the reason.

This reminds us of the true saying 'when the reason is known, there will be no wonder'. If someone says to you, for example, 'My father confessor prevented me from talking to so and so', do not be amazed thinking that the father confessor creates quarrels. Perhaps if you knew the reason, you would know that that person is a stumbling block to another and causes him to sin, causes him irritation, or encourages bad thoughts. In other words, having friendship with him comes within the scope of the verse, *"Evil company corrupts good habits"* (1 Cor. 15:33), or the verse, *"Put away from yourselves that wicked person"* (1 Cor. 5:13), or the words of the Psalmist : *"Blessed is the man. Who walks not in the counsel of the ungodly, Nor stands in the path of sinners, Nor sits in the seat of the scornful"* (Ps. 1).

The principle: Half facts are not facts, apply to theological matters as well.

An example of this is the case of using one verse and ignoring other verses relating to the same subject by which full understanding of doctrine can be realized. For example a person may speak about faith alone saying it is written, *"Believe on the Lord Jesus Christ, and you will be saved, you and our household"* (Acts 16:31).

We answer such a person, saying, 'use this verse in conjunction with the words of the Lord, *"He who believes and is baptized will be saved"* (Mark 16:16), and the words of St. Peter the Apostle to the Jews on the Day of Pentecost, *"Repent, and let ever one of you be baptized in the name of Jesus Christ for the remission of sin; and you shall receive the gift of the Holy Spirit"* (Acts 2:38).'

So, when anyone says to you: 'It is written so and so...', answer him: 'It is also written so and so...'

This is the clear way of debating and refuting thoughts which the Lord Christ used in the temptation on the Mount. This is the way by which truth represents the whole fact, otherwise, if anything is concealed the fact will be misunderstood.

People's rights:

Another meaning for truth is related to people's rights.

It is therefore said: Give everyone his right. And hence came the expression "human rights". Previously the Ministry of Justice was called "The Ministry of Lawful Rights" and the Faculty of Law in Arabic is called, 'Faculty of Rights' as the law relates to people's rights and obligations.

The opposite to the word "right" here is iniquity by which rights are lost.

It refers to what is due and what is not.

It refers to what one has the right to do and not to do, just as the thief on the right hand of the Lord on the cross said to the other thief, *"And we indeed justly, for we receive the due reward of our deeds"* (Luke 23:41).

Hence also came the word *"worthy to partake of the holy sacraments"*, or *"eats in an unworthy manner"* (1Cor. 11:27), that is, no one has the right to partake of the holy sacraments if they are not repentant and do not have purity of heart.

Perhaps this was what the lost son meant when he said to his father, *"I.. am no longer worthy to be called your*

119

son" (Luke 15:21), and also, *"a worker is worthy of his food"* (Matt. 10:10), (Luke 10:7).

Truth versus Falsehood:

Another concept of truth is connected with its being opposite to falsity.

True gold is other than false gold, and a true marriage, that is, a lawful marriage is opposite to an unlawful marriage. And it is said of the Lord Christ that He is *"the true Light"* (John 1:9), and of John the Baptist that ,*"He was not that Light, but was sent to bear witness of that Light"* (John 1:8).

The Lord Christ said about Himself, *"I am the light of the world. He who follows Me shall not walk in darkness"* (John 8:12). And He said to us, *"You are the light of the world"* (Matt. 5:14). Even though He called us the light, He is the true Light because He is Himself light whereas we see light only through His light. The light of the sun is true light, whereas the light of the moon is not because it is mere reflection of the sun's light on it. Without the light of the sun, the moon becomes dark.

The meaning here is true and genuine and can be applied to many examples.

A person may say that he is the spiritual son of a certain priest, but in fact he is not because he does not obey or consult him.

Someone may say that he has repented whereas he is not repenting, because every time he repents, he returns again to sin.

Another person may say that he always prays, but in fact he does not pray, because he talks to God with his mouth only and his heart is far from him.

Or a person who says that he is fasting but in actual fact he is not; he is a vegetarian who cares to make his food delicious. Such a person has no self control during fasting and is not considered fasting according to the spiritual rules of fast.

With regard to God, He is the only true God (John 17:3).

Many were called gods, however, this was merely a title, for they were not truly gods. Take for example what is stated in the Psalms: *"God stands in the congregation of the might; He judges among the gods"* (Ps. 82:1). And, *"I said, 'You are gods, and all of you are children of the Most High. But you shall die like men..."* (Ps. 82:6,7).

The Lord said also to Moses, *"See, I have made you as God to Pharaoh"* (Ex. 7:1). *"As God" here means to be master, not to be Creator, Almighty or Omnipresent. And it is said also that "all the gods of the peoples are idols"* (Ps. 96:5). This is the difference between truth and falsity.

The same distinction was made by St. Paul the Apostle concerning widows.

He said, *"do not let the church be burdened, that it may relieve those who are really widows"* (1 Tim. 5:16).

The same can be said regarding a true believer and children of God.

Many are called God's children and pray, saying, "Our Father who are in heaven", yet they are not real children; for the words of St. John the Apostle do not apply to them: *"Whoever has been born of God does not sin," "and the wicked one does not touch him," "and he cannot sin, because he has been born of God"* (1 John 3:9; 5:18).

The words of the Apostle about the Lord do not apply to such people, *"If you know that He is righteous, you know that everyone who practices righteousness is born of Him"* (1 John 2:29).

St. James the Apostle says about the person who says that he is a believer but does not demonstrate his faith through works, *"But do you want to know, O foolish man, that faith without works is dead?"* (James 2:20).

St. Paul the Apostle says very serious words, *"Examine yourselves as to whether you are in the faith. prove yourselves"* (2 Corinthians 13:5).

See also what hard words the Lord said to the angel of the Church in Sardis, *"You have a name that you are alive, but you are dead"* (Rev. 3:1).

The word "alive" here is not the true name which that angel deserved; for he was not really alive but spiritually dead.

The truth begins with the principles or values which a person observes in life.

Whatever conforms with sound spiritual values is truth, and whatever conforms with sound theological doctrines is right and the opposite is false and vain.

Truth lost:

Truth is opposed to hypocrisy.

Hypocrisy is against reality because it involves falsehood and the interior is different from the exterior. Therefore the Lord Christ reprimanded the scribes and Pharisees as hypocrites because they were like whitewashed tombs which indeed appear beautiful outwardly, but inside are full of dead men's bones and all uncleanness (Matt. 23:27).

The hypocrite shows himself to be something different from what he really is.

Flattery also is against truth:

Flattery is praising another person insincerely to please him or to defend him whereas the fact is different and what the flatterer thinks or feels in his heart is the opposite of what he says.

The truth is also lost under the pretext of courtesy or (love).

Or rather under the name of false love, as when a person pretends that he is a friend to someone and leads him to ruin or encourages him to do something wrong. His insincere encouragement may cause his friend to continue doing wrong. Under the pretense of love - which is false love - he ruins his friend completely.

There is also a mother who - thinking that she loves her son - spoils him. Her love is not true love.

Also a youth may pretend that he loves a girl while his relation with her is mere lust without love. Under the pretext of love he may spoil her reputation and ruin her life. This is not love in its true meaning since it has no principles.

Here we mention also those who falsely defend people who do wrong. They forget the words of the Scriptures: *"He who justifies the wicked, and he who condemns the just, both of them alike are an abomination to the Lord"* (Prov. 17:15).

The reason is that both of these work against the truth. Some may not like the expression "condemns the just" and think it unfair. But in fact people often disregard one's faults and consider him innocent, feeling some sort of compassion and mercy, even though they work against truth. If this person's compassion was sincere, it would have lead the sinner to repentance.

On the other hand justifying the wicked will not make him realize his fault, and therefore he will continue in his way without repentance and hence the person who justified him would have done him harm.

However, someone may justify a wicked person out of ignorance.

Yet he is also an abomination to the Lord. My advice to such a person is: **Defend the truth instead of defending persons.**

If you defend someone, you may be deviating from the truth.

In order to defend the truth, you ought to know it. Many people do not have such knowledge and may follow rumours or take knowledge from people who do not have the true knowledge.

Some may claim that they are defending the truth whereas they are in fact far from it.

Another person may defend the truth - or what he thinks is the truth - in a way so far from the truth.

He may go beyond what he is allowed to say or defame someone, condemn him, cause harm and hurt the feelings of others, or spread false information. In this case he would have done so much wrong against others and committed sin that God will condemn him.

He may argue that he is defending the truth even though it is in an illegitimate way!

Therefore, if you want to hold on to the truth, ignore rumours and do not trust every statement you hear. Remember also that who is against the truth is against God Himself, and the reason is that :

God is Truth, absolute Truth.

Truth is God:

The Lord Christ - glory be to him - said, *"And you shall know the Truth, and the Truth shall make you free"* (John 8:32); and also, *"I am the way, the truth, and the life"* (John 14:6). So whoever keeps away from truth, keeps far away from God, and here lies the danger.

A truthful person is a person who lives according to values and principles. A truthful person has God's Spirit in him because God's Spirit is *"the Spirit of truth"* (John 14:17; 15,26). Whoever keeps away from truth keeps away from God's Spirit, and whoever separates himself from the truth separates himself from God.

A truthful person does not measure with two elements; one for his beloved and the other for others, or else he will have separated himself from the truth.

The devil separated himself from God's communion, so the Lord *said "he is a liar and the father of it"* (John 8:44), *"He was a murderer from the beginning, and does not stand in the truth, because there is no truth in him"* (John 8:44).

See also how Ananias and Sapphira were punished for their lie. St. Peter said to Ananias, *"You have not lied to men but to God"* (Acts 5:4).

CHAPTER TEN

THE CONCEPT OF KNOWLEDGE

God gave us a mind that can receive knowledge.

But He wanted us to know what is useful and of benefit to us, and also what may be of use and benefit to others; whether individuals or groups.

However, the problem that faced man from the beginning was that he wanted to know everything, even to know evil. The first man knew only good, but when he ate from the tree of the knowledge of good and evil he knew also evil and thus caused harm to himself.

Be sure of the soundness of any knowledge you receive. Be sure of its benefit before accepting it.

Know also that knowledge is not a goal in itself but a means for your benefit. So choose this kind of useful knowledge.

Kinds of knowledge:

There is a sensuous knowledge which comes to a person through senses. People know it by sight, touch, smell or hearing. Another kind of knowledge comes through the mind by study or inference.

Some knowledge is a kind of divine manifestation or divine revelation:

God reveals to His holy people what He wants them to know. He does this through the Holy Spirit of which it is said in the Book of Isaiah the Prophet, *"the Spirit of wisdom and understanding... the Spirit of knowledge"* (Is.11:2).

This was the knowledge the Psalmist requested in his prayers : *"Show me Your ways, O Lord, teach me Your paths"* (Ps. 25:4).

It is the best knowledge of which we say in the Liturgy of St. Gregory, 'You have given me the ability to know You'. Of this knowledge also the Lord Christ said in His soliloquy with the Father, *"And this is eternal life, that they may know You, the only true God... "* (John 17:3), and also, *"O righteous Father! The world has not known You, but I have known You... "* (John 17:25). In regards to granting His disciples divine knowledge, *"And I have declared to them Your name, and will declare it, that the love with which You loved Me may be in them, and I in them"* (John 17:26).

It is then the knowledge which leads to God's love and to God's dwelling in us.

A scientist is fond of seeking knowledge that gives an idea, for example, about the moon and planets by manufacturing very expensive spaceships, his fondness to know God is much less. He becomes very happy when he brings some stones from the moon or even some photos, because these give some knowledge about nature which is God's creation without enjoying God Himself.

The same can be said about many of the discoveries of man.

There is knowledge that comes from other sources.

It may come through books, newspapers, films, or other varied mass media. Knowledge may also come from friends or colleagues.

There is knowledge that comes through the devil.

The devil may cast such knowledge into the minds of people as he did with Eve. The devil may also give certain knowledge through a thought, a dream or through one of his supporters. The knowledge he gives may be false knowledge. It may also be true knowledge but the devil uses it for evil purposes.

A person may seek to obtain knowledge from the devil through magic, calling up the dead or the spirits or by any other means which the divine revelation prohibited, *"There shall not be found among you... Who practices witchcraft, or a soothsayer, or one who interprets omens, or a sorcerer, or one who conjures spells, or a medium, or a spiritist, or one who calls up the dead. For all who do these things are an abomination to the Lord... "* (Deut. 18:10,11).

King Saul was an example of those who fell into this sin when he sought knowledge from a woman who was a medium at En Dor (1 Sam. 28:7)

Other examples also are those who seek soothsayers, palmists or clairvoyants, or those who read coffee cup, call up spirits through hypnotism and the like; all of which are described by God as *"abominations of nations"* (Deut. 18:9,12).

How do you know that such knowledge you obtain is truth and will not be used to lead you astray?

Know then that any information given to you by the devil is not freely given, nor without a wicked purpose to harm you or to put you under his authority and leadership.

Another kind of knowledge is knowing yourself.

"Know yourself" is a wise saying by Socrates the Philosopher.

You can gain great benefits from knowing yourself. When you know that you are dust and ash, you will be humbled. When you are aware of your sins, you will be regretful, repentful and contrite. When you know your nature and the wars within you, you will be able to overcome them. And when you know your talents, you will use them to glorify God.

There is also the knowledge of God's Holy Scriptures and Commandments.

St. Paul the Apostle said to his disciple St. Timothy, *"from childhood you have known the Holy Scriptures, which are able to make you wise for salvation through faith... "* (2 Tim. 3:15). This Scripture *"is profitable for doctrine, for reproof, for correction, for instruction in righteousness"* (2 Tim. 3:16).

Through knowing this Scripture, you will know the Lord's path and know how the saints walked it.

With such knowledge you will have wisdom and discernment.

You will know what is good for you and you will discern God's path from the devils deception and craftiness. And when you know this, *"you will save both yourself and those who hear you"* (1 Tim. 4:16).

Through this knowledge you will be able to discern spirits as St. John the Apostle said, *"Do not believe every spirit, but test the spirits, whether they are of God; because many false prophets have gone out into the world"* (1 John 4:1).

Know others in order to know how to deal with them.

This applies to friendship, whether it be at work, socially, or within the family. You ought to know and be aware of the differing personalities and characters so that you may best know how to deal with each person. You should be aware of how to deal with adults, as well as understanding the nature of children.

Also, it is important to be aware of the psychology of, say, the handicapped, the retarded, the orphaned, the barren, and so on, so that you may best deal with each one accordingly.

Know God, and know that He sees you wherever you go.

God knows your thoughts, your intentions, your desires and your sins. If you know this, you will be ashamed of every wicked thought or lustful desire. Put before you the words which God repeats in all His messages to the angels of the seven churches in Asia, *"I know your works"* (Rev. 2:2).

This knowledge is capable of bringing God's fear into your heart.

Be keen on knowing truth, and when you know it follow it.

How beautiful are the words of David the Prophet in the Psalm, *"Open my eyes, that I may see ... Turn away my eyes from looking at worthless things"* (Ps. 119:18,37).

Try also to know the needs of people so that you may be able to provide for them.

Try to know the way of salvation, to walk its path and lead others onto the path as well.

Be aware of knowledge which may be beyond your spiritual level.

About this Job the Prophet said, *"I have uttered what I did not understand, things too wonderful for me, which I did not know"* (Job 42:3).

Many people search theological matters beyond their spiritual level, so they deviate. Others search matters relating to the world of spirits and their thoughts lead them astray. You ought then to be humble. Search only matters that lead you to your salvation.

Harmful knowledge:

Some knowledge is very harmful like that in which our father Adam and our mother Eve fell. It led them to lose their innocence and simplicity and live in the dualism of good and evil, truth and falsity, the lawful and the unlawful. Their children lived and still live in this dualism up to the present day.

True then are the words of the Wise Solomon in the book of Ecclesiastes, *"For in much wisdom is much grief"* (Eccl. 1:18).

These words relate to the knowledge of harmful things that are of no benefit to a person, but may actually cause him harm. At times he may claim that such knowledge is merely general knowledge, not realizing its danger!

Therefore one of the spiritual fathers said the following beneficial words : 'Sometimes we make an effort to know things for which we shall not be condemned on the Day of Judgment for ignorance thereof . If we are not to be condemned for not knowing these matters, how much rather shall we be condemned for knowing things that are harmful for us and that have a bad impact on us?'

Keep in mind the consequences of such harmful knowledge.

Whatever knowledge comes to your mind will affect your senses and feelings, and will affect your relationship with others. Moreover, such knowledge will be stored in your subconscious.

This knowledge will affect and influence your subconscious in the form of suspicions, thoughts or dreams. It will extend within you and outside to a great extent and you may not be able to stop it or its harmful effects.

Therefore we should use our intellect in accepting only matters which are of benefit to us and to others.

Many people wept and regretted knowledge which have been stored in their minds.

They wished they would have not known such things whether by reading about it or experiencing through the senses. They feel at a loss as to how to remove such knowledge from their minds after it being implanted in them.

An example is those who fall into drug addiction, and are unable to get out of it.

Some kind of knowledge changes one's look to various matters and even to certain people.

Our mother Eve, after taking the harmful, deceitful knowledge from the serpent, changed her perception towards the tree of the knowledge of good and evil, which was in the midst of the garden and which she perhaps was everyday.

After such knowledge, Eve *"saw that the tree was good for food, that it was pleasant to the eyes, and a tree desirable to make one wise"* (Gen. 3:6).

After her perception towards the tree changed, lust entered into her heart to eat of it. So, *"she took of its fruit and ate. She also gave to her husband with her, and he ate."*

Another kind of harmful knowledge is doubt. A scientist once said, **'It is easy for doubt to enter one's mind. But it is difficult to cast it out.'**

So, if you give an ear to someone who throws doubt in your heart regarding a certain person, by making false accusations, or if you indulge in reading harmful material which might make you suspicious concerning your faith or the Scriptures, you will have to exert much effort to rid yourself of such suspicions. This doubtfulness might last a long time, until God's grace visits you and relieves you of your suspicions.

A person should, therefore, be careful in choosing the source of his knowledge.

Keep your mind pure and do not blot it with harmful knowledge. Be very careful regarding what you read, hear or see; and be careful in choosing the friends who impart knowledge or bring you harmful experiences, harmful information or inappropriate thoughts. Do not let such knowledge abide in your mind except after being completely assured of it and after ascertaining what is true and what is false.

Do not think that thoughts are of no concern, for thoughts often bring forth many other thoughts.

One word which comes to your mind may, for example, produce a story or more. Know then that protecting oneself from a thought is much better than accepting it and later having to rid yourself of it.

Be very careful regarding the transfer of knowledge and thoughts.

Some harmful knowledge may come to you, and you by turn transfer it to another and cause him harm. After suffering from this knowledge, you try to rid yourself of it, and by God's grace you do, however, what about the other person you have relayed this harmful information to? You will be condemned for the harm you caused to the other person. In this case, your sin did not harmed you but has harmed the person you transferred that harmful knowledge to.

It is your past which follows you; the harmful knowledge you have spread, whether by speech, writing or other means.

Those who commit the sin of judging and belittling others by conveying wrong things about them, or speaking about their mistakes, will be tortured by their conscience which may awaken them and reprove them for what they had done.

This applies also to those who invent or spread rumours for the intention of either harming others, or simply for sinful amusement. They speak about the secrets of other people, and may even add their imagination to the story.

Knowledge of trivialities:

Your brain is like a computer with a certain capacity for collecting data.

So, you ought not occupy a large part of it with trivialities which may hinder from storing useful things.

Keep only what you need or what is necessary for your life, and serves a useful purpose, and know that whatever you keep in your mind will certainly be revealed whether intentionally or unintentionally. There may be some information kept in your subconscience some years ago and you find them coming out unexpectedly on any occasion you are not prepared for.

Some use their minds in collecting futile and vain knowledge.

This may not be in itself a sin, but such knowledge occupies the mind with trivialities and distracts it from spiritual and theological matters.

It thus hinders the mind from positive work which builds your spiritual life and prevents the mind from useful contemplations.

These people may also transfer such trivial knowledge to others.

They transfer it through their conversation with others which is of no benefit. It is merely the wasting of time which can be used in other productive things.

I wish you would only occupy your mind with constructive knowledge which would help strengthen your personality, elevate your feelings and promote your spiritualities, and which will be useful to humanity or to the community in which you live.